LESLIE A. WILCOX
R.I., R.S.M.A.

THIS EDITION IS LIMITED
TO SIX HUNDRED COPIES ONLY

LESLIE A. WILCOX

R.I., R.S.M.A.

---

by

FRANK G. G. CARR, C.B., C.B.E.

Former Director,
National Maritime Museum, Greenwich

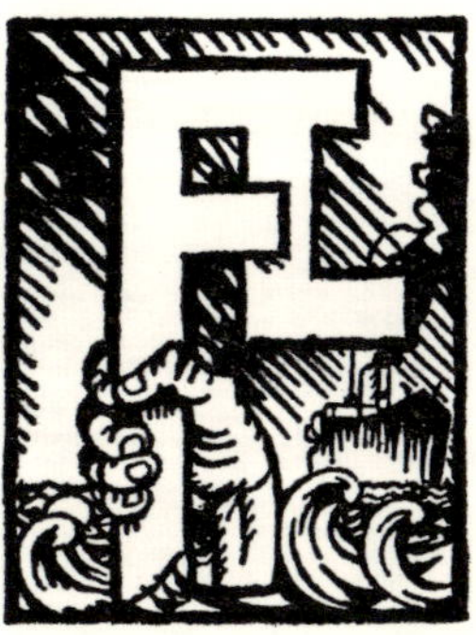

F. LEWIS, PUBLISHERS, LIMITED

PUBLISHERS BY APPOINTMENT TO THE LATE QUEEN MARY

LEIGH-ON-SEA

PRINTED AND MADE IN ENGLAND

SBN 85317 049 5

First Published 1977

PRODUCED UNDER THE SUPERVISION OF THE PUBLISHERS AT
DAEDALUS PRESS, STOKE FERRY, NORFOLK

Table of Contents

ERRATUM

Catalogue

Page 28 Catalogue no. 115 *for* 1860 *read* 1861

Illustrations

Catalogue no. 128 *for* Canvas 29 x 40 *read* 28 x 40 ins.
Catalogue no. 198 *for* Canvas 19 x 13 *read* 19 x 36 ins.

Acknowledgments

The author and publishers wish to express their thanks and indebtedness to those who, in various ways, have given the valuable assistance that has made this record possible. Special thanks are due to Mr. Bertram Newbury, of the Parker Gallery, London, the artist's Agents, without whose co-operation this book would have been impossible, as this firm control all copyrights as sole agents of the artist.

Preface

OF LESLIE WILCOX it may truthfully be said that he is, like the great Van de Veldes, essentially a sailor's artist. His work is not only pleasing when judged by the highest standards of art as such, but it also never fails to satisfy the critical eye of the seaman. This whether he be the 'Old Shellback' who has served his time in sail, or the 'Fisherman of England' admiring one of the evocative pictures that he has so generously painted year after year for the Christmas cards of the Royal National Mission to Deep Sea Fishermen.

This cannot be said of all marine artists. To elaborate, there is a quality about Turner's incomparable sea pieces that is unique; but it tends to be of a Wagnerian character, as in such pictures as his immortal 'Fighting Temeraire'. The effect is superb, but the maritime record faulty, even to the extent that to heighten the drama the sun is shown conveniently setting in the east.

The story is also told of another of his famous paintings, the magnificent 'Battle of Trafalgar' now in the National Maritime Museum, but formerly one of the show pieces in the Painted Hall at Greenwich. A group of visitors, conducted by an old Naval pensioner, was standing before it, spellbound in admiration. 'Yes', admitted their ancient cicerone, himself a veteran of the great battle, 'That's all right as far as it goes, but we did ought to 'ave 'ad 'uggins'. Breath-taking as was Turner's power to stir the emotions, to the sailor who had been there, his ships were a fantasy. Painted by W. J. Huggins, they would have been real.

It is the rare genius of Wilcox that he can both seize and visualise the drama as brilliantly as if he himself had been present and witnessed with his own eyes the events that he depicts so accurately, while at the same time painting the ships in all their glory as they truly were; ships that seamen could sail and handle, real ships, not just stage properties, however beautiful. In his ability to do this he is unsurpassed by any other living artist.

Samuel Pepys would have liked his pictures. He would have revelled in this book. Had it been published three hundred years ago, it would have found an honoured place in his Library, now at Magdalene College, Cambridge. To-day we would regard this as additional evidence for the diarist's discerning taste in art.

'Ships and the sea,' wrote Masefield, 'There's nothing finer made'; and one senses instinctively of Wilcox that as he doggedly developed his outstanding talent, it was increasingly this belief, ever more deeply felt, that has inspired his finest work. Beyond all shadow of doubt, by sheer merit alone, he has won his place among the great marine artists of all time, not just of this age alone; and his work will continue to be sought out and cherished for as long as men love ships and the sea.

Introduction

'His pipe between his lips;
Still, dreaming, seems to see
The lost and lovely ships
That no one sees but he.'
(C. Fox Smith)

AN ARTIST who sells every single painting in his own one-man exhibition is fortunate; but to sell all of them in three days is truly remarkable even though the exhibition in question takes place in one of the best London art centres. Leslie Wilcox, whose paintings were swept up in this way, is well known for his interest in the sea and ships, particularly the magnificent clipper ships, the study of which has fascinated sailors and 'landlubbers' from early times.

The importance of the sailing ship began to decline about the middle of the last century when steamships had already begun to dominate the scene; but the saga of the sailing ship, especially of the fully rigged 'three-master', the splendour of her appearance and the skill and courage of those who sailed in her, will never fail to be subjects of admiration.

Wilcox must have been moved by such feelings when he first embarked on his varied career for, as will be seen, his work as a marine painter is notable not only for his evident technical knowledge but for his happy knack of capturing the narrative element in all his canvases. He must have given intensive study to the construction, sail plan and rig of the clipper ship, for his paintings reveal an acute observation which enabled him to place his vessel firmly in the water, carrying just the right amount of sail for the conditions prevailing. Many artists dealing with such subjects have fallen into the trap of overdoing the picturesque, depicting a theatrical, over-canvassed ship ploughing through seas of dramatic magnitude which would result in disaster in no time at all. Not so in the Wilcox compositions, and there is no doubt that his understanding of the sea and ships, together with his studied avoidance of unreality, contributed greatly to his success.

It is generally agreed that much of his accuracy is due to the fact that he used models in painting the great ships; at any rate we know there was a time in earlier life when all kinds of model-making held his attention. The importance he attached to accuracy in this art was practically demonstrated in 1947. It was then that, in association with the late Commander Crane, the first editor of *Ships and Ship Models,* who writing under the pen-name of 'Jason' was widely read by ship lovers the world over, he founded the

'Guild of Model Shipwrights'. Unlike the artist, the model maker works in three dimensions, and he cannot ignore some detail on which he is doubtful by concealing it conveniently behind the bulwarks. His work must be both complete and correct.

The Guild, like the ancient Guilds of the City of London, was founded with twin aims, both of which it successfully achieved. First, it was established to set standards of quality and accuracy to which all accepted members must adhere. Secondly, and directly stemming from this, it obtained for them the status and dignity of a recognised craft. The results of Wilcox's pioneer work in this are seen today in *The Model Shipwright*; a hard-backed technical journal that has appeared quarterly since the autumn of 1972 under the able editorship of Arthur L. Tucker.

It might be appropriate also to mention here his skill as a carver in wood. When in 1956 the late Edward Bowness, editor of *Model Ships and Power Boats,* insisted that the figurehead of the 'Cutty Sark' was a replacement of the original lost at sea, and was crudely unworthy of the ship that it adorned – a statement later discovered to be ill-founded – it was to Wilcox that an appeal was made to carve a model that would serve as a pattern for a new figure which would be more in keeping with the high standards of Hellyer of Blackwall, who had been responsible for the creation of that supposed to have been lost. The large scale model thereupon produced by Leslie Wilcox was, as was only to be expected, both enchanting in form and exquisite in workmanship; and it is greatly to be regretted that the professional figurehead carver employed, on the recommendation of Bowness, to carry out the full-sized work, wilfully ignored the Wilcox model and unfortunately followed his own not altogether happy ideas, with the result that may be assessed by all who visit the ship at Greenwich today.

The use of models also enabled Wilcox to paint ships of different periods so that, almost by chance, he has become an historian of the events surrounding them. It was this attention to important detail that led to the acceptance of his modelling work by the Science Museum, the Liverpool Museum, and Trinity House.

Leslie Arthur Wilcox, born in London in 1904, is essentially a modest man, unaffected by the success he has achieved. The youngest of his family, he was encouraged by his parents to develop a variety of hobbies which served him in good stead in later life. Instead of the luxuries of life and the careless contacts of friends he seems to have preferred the workshop and the delight of making things.

Very early his restless curiosity turned to the study of the motor car and in fact, about the time of World War I he tried to get a job in a local motor firm but without success. Foiled in this attempt, however, he began to draw cars, and aeroplanes as well, and eventually reached the stage when he felt able to send some of his work to an advertising studio in the Strand where in a few days he obtained his first job for which he was paid the princely sum of five shillings per week. This included instruction in the art of lettering together with other subjects necessary to the commercial artist. Sensibly he never remained in one studio for too long, realising that experience in a number of subjects, rather than specialisation in one, would improve his technical abilities.

His extraordinary versatility as a skilled craftsman and the variety of his interests was strikingly demonstrated in 1937, when he successfully tackled the daunting task of making himself an astronomical telescope. This was no mere toy, but the complete construction of a Newtonian reflector, from the grinding, polishing and silvering of the six-inch mirror to the detailed precision of the equatorial mounting. And it worked. Both optically and mechanically it was excellent; a truly remarkable achievement.

The years passed in this way, the young man becoming conversant with many activities in different commerical studios but, at last, came the decision to launch out on his own.

It was not a very good time to start, seeing that the country had gone off the gold standard and was deep in the throes of an economic slump; but, in spite of the fact that he was soon losing business and beginning to despair (for at that time there was no social service or aid for the self-employed), he did have a stroke of good luck in meeting an illustrator who persuaded him to try his hand at this special kind of work even though it involved a large amount of figure drawing at which he was not particularly adept. It is a tribute to his character and determination that he managed, nevertheless, to get an order which kept him reasonably secure financially until the beginning of World War II.

The war naturally curtailed any further progress; for there was an immediate shortage of paper which was strictly rationed for essential purposes and, of course, advertising and editorial work declined as time went on.

Leslie Wilcox had recently married and started a family but with only a reduced income and uncertain prospects he volunteered into the Naval Patrol Service as an Ordinary Seaman, later being seconded to Naval Camouflage making models of ships, which revived the original skills of his youth. It was while he was working in this Department that, in 1940, the forty United States 'moth-balled' four-funnel destroyers of World War I, the famous four-stackers that became our Town Class, were transferred to the Royal Navy under the Lease-Lend arrangements to provide the additional escorts which the Atlantic convoys so desperately needed at that most critical stage in the nation's fortunes. Unhappily the Admiralty had no plans or detailed information on the ships that they were about to receive. It was singularly fortunate, therefore, that Wilcox was able to fill the gap from his own extensive maritime records. He remembered that completely detailed plans of the class had been prepared for model makers and published in the American *Popular Science Monthly* in 1927, and that he had in his library at home the complete set of all the relevant issues. These he was able to produce, and did so, to the considerable surprise and great satisfaction of Their Lordships. It is needless to stress the value that the Admiralty placed on this wholly unexpected and most welcome contribution.

During this time he met Frank Mason, R.I., who was serving in the same Department of the Navy, and it is easy to imagine that this friendship was a welcome one, seeing that it provided the means of exchanging notes on matters of mutual interest. Any time then left to Wilcox between his Naval war duties was spent contributing illustrations to yachting journals, and by the time hostilities ceased, this particular work had become a regular form of employment.

Shortly after the war he began his painting career, sending in one or two paintings to the newly formed Society of Marine Artists, one of which, much to his surprise, was accepted and subsequently sold. As one might expect this success encouraged him to do more and in 1947 he was elected to membership of the Society, where, with few exceptions, he has exhibited each year since.

In 1960, he became the Honorary Secretary, an onerous and responsible post which he held until he resigned in 1974, when he moved out of London to a house in the country at Rustington, in Sussex. Two important developments in the history of the Society, with both of which he was intimately concerned, took place during his tenure of office. Of these, the first was the fulfilment of its plans to establish a Diploma Collection, to which all members were desired to contribute an example of their work. This was formed in 1966, when it was also arranged that the pictures comprising the Collection should be permanently housed in the National Maritime Museum at Greenwich.

Nothing could have been more entirely appropriate, and the Museum authorities as their part of a bargain so mutually advantageous to both sides, undertook to exhibit from time to time as might be most suitable selections of pictures from the Collection. There is no doubt that H.R.H. The Duke of Edinburgh, who already owned a number of paintings by Wilcox, and who was a member of the Museum's Board of Trustees, would have welcomed this scheme. Perhaps it is not entirely a coincidence that shortly after this, the Society was accorded the privilege of adding the word Royal to its title, to be known thereafter as the Royal Society of Marine Artists.

Wilcox is too modest to speak of his own part in securing this most welcome recognition of the importance which should rightly be accorded to the work of marine artists as a whole; but one suspects that painstaking care and tactful diplomacy on the part of the Honorary Secretary had much to do with this success.

It appears that in the first years of his membership nearly all his paintings were executed in water colour, which accounts for his becoming, in due course, a member of the well established Royal Institute of Painters in Water Colour, a privilege he enjoyed until he finally decided to paint in oils. All these achievements must have brought great satisfaction, and there were times when he would look back thankfully to his good fortune in having tried his hand at so many interesting things.

During the 1950s, commissions, the hallmark of an established artist, started to come his way and among these were paintings commemorating naval and military occasions, and even some portraits, one of which, of H.M. the Queen Mother, was commissioned by the Black Watch (Royal Highland Regiment) of Canada. Other portraits included one of Lord Lugard, the first Governor of Nigeria and several for Durham University, including Sir James Hunt for Grey College, and Professor Eric Birley for Hatfield College. Then came a painting symbolising thecontinuous union between the Royal Navy and the Royal Naval Volunteer Reserve which showed H.M.S. Warspite, with a Guided Missile Destroyer alongside, and the Royal yacht Britannia and in front the R.N.V.R. Sailing Club's yacht The Volunteer. This work he presented to the R.N.V.R. Club. His painting of H.M. the Queen Mother receiving the Freedom of the Musicians Company from the Master, Mr. G. D. Lockett, splendidly records this great event in the annals of the Company.

Then came workmanlike military paintings, including the First Battalion the Royal Hampshire Regiment, under heavy shell fire, landing on the beach at Le Hamel on 6th June 1944 and, separated historically by almost two hundred years, the Battle of Bunker Hill, viewed from above the American position.

But his real ambition, more than once fulfilled, was to paint large historical marine pictures. The first of these he did for his own satisfaction and the size of this canvas by today's standards is indeed very large. The subject was 'Mr. Pepys' Navy'. His next was painted for Liberty's of Regent Street, London, namely 'The Prince of Wales leaving Plymouth for North America in 1861'. This was followed by 'Jeannette', details of which are included in the catalogue of his works. Paintings of this kind were necessarily often left on the easel for a considerable time whilst the artist proceeded with urgent commissions.

About the year 1950 Wilcox produced a *Boy's Book of Ships* for Blackie's, which contains about twenty-four pictures of ships and during the ensuing years a series of book jackets was undertaken. In 1963 Geo. Bell & Co., for whom some of these jackets were designed, asked whether he had ever considered writing a book. As a matter of fact he had, like many people, toyed with the idea but, aware of some of his limitations in this respect, had decided against it. However, he was pressed into the preparation of a synopsis as a result of which a book was published entitled *Mr. Pepys' Navy*. Later there came *Anson's Voyage* in 1969.

Both these books were not only written and illustrated by him, but for the actual printing he undertook additionally the detailed planning, make-up and production of each volume, including the layout and design of every page. The resulting harmony of line drawings and text is a delight to the eye and one that every discerning reader may enjoy; but it also demonstrates dramatically the author's sympathy for and understanding of the printer's art.

The large painting 'Mr. Pepys' Navy' found an American buyer and the 'Mayflower and Speedwell at Dartmouth' was bought by the Pilgrim Society, Plymouth, Mass.

In 1961 he spent five weeks in Jamaica making sketches and taking notes for a brochure on a holiday complex there – probably this work was proposed because, a year or two before, two paintings had been commissioned by Government House in Jamaica. It was during his 1961 visit that he put together a portfolio of twenty small oil sketches for an exhibition, but unfortunately the whereabouts of these are unknown.

But of all the commissions received the one giving the greatest satisfaction was that which was commissioned by the present Queen to depict the return from the Commonwealth Tour of 1953. This painting now hangs in the Royal yacht Britannia. Other important works included three paintings for His Royal Highness the Duke of Edinburgh, and a large canvas for the South African Ambassador. Senators Humphrey and McGovern of the United States possess examples of his work also, and he is represented by several paintings in the National Maritime Museum, Greenwich.

In 1972 Wilcox contributed an illustrated article to *The Connoisseur* featuring the exquisite bone ship models worked mostly by French prisoners of the Napoleonic Wars and comparing these with models of more recent date. Twenty years earlier he had written an interesting account of the full scale model he made for the Corporation of Trinity House of the ship called the Loyal London. When Trinity House was burned as the result of enemy action on the memorable night of December 30-31, 1940, one of the largest of the Stuart period ship models, a contemporary model of the Loyal London, which was one of the Corporation's most treasured possessions, was completely destroyed. The Loyal London, a gift from the City of London, was built by Captain John Taylor, and launched at Deptford in 1666. She took part in the Second Dutch War, and during the course of an action off Chatham was burned by the Dutch on June 13th, 1667. Admiral Sir Jeremy Smyth, who had been Captain of the Loyal London, and was an Elder Brother of Trinity House, asked Jonas Shish – a Master Shipwright at Deptford and in charge of the dockyard – to build a model of her for Trinity House. This model was acquired by Trinity House in 1673, and was treasured by the Corporation until its destruction in 1940.

In 1943 a start was made by Robert Spence, an authority on ships of the Stuart period, and Leslie Wilcox on a model of the Loyal London to replace the contemporary one. This work was completed in 1951 and an account of this appeared in the *Illustrated London News,* April 21, 1951.

It was at this time that Wilcox became associated with the Parker Gallery of Albemarle Street, London, an establishment harking back to the eighteenth century, for whom he produced over the years many of his famous paintings of clipper ships and other marine pictures. April, 1973, saw his remarkable one-man exhibition there which, as it happened, broke a two-century tradition, the Gallery never before having mounted an exhibition of the works of a living artist. As already mentioned, all his paintings were sold in three days on this occasion. Another one-man show was organised in 1976 in conjunction with Wm. Blair Inc, of Bethesda, Maryland, the paintings depicting incidents at sea during the first year of the American War of Independence, 1776. Here again there was a number of enthusiastic American buyers at the pre-view when a third of the exhibits were sold overnight.

Meanwhile, between 1973 and 1976 Wilcox was steadily painting famous Clippers for the Parker Gallery's many patrons of his works; and one commission worthy of mention was a painting of the aircraft carrier Valley Forge at Hong Kong at the outbreak of the Korean War. This was presented by the American patron to the Valley Forge Military Academy at Wayne.

A more recent historical picture is of 'Nelson's flagship H.M.S. Vanguard arriving at Naples after the Battle of the Nile'. This was exhibited at the R.S.M.A. 1976 exhibition and had the place of honour amongst the numerous paintings on view.

With his meticulous research into historical detail, his romantic outlook and feeling for sky and sea, it can be said that there is no artist working in Britain today who matches his ability to put marine history on to canvas and make a picture of it.

CATALOGUE

Catalogue Abbreviations

Auct.	Auctioned
c.	circa
Exhib.	Exhibited
H.M.	Her Majesty
H.M.S.	Her Majesty's Ship
H.R.H.	His Royal Highness
M.S.	Motor Ship
Repr.	Reproduced
R.B.A.	Royal Society of British Artists
R.I.	Royal Institute of Painters in Water Colours
R.O.I.	Royal Institute of Oil Painters
R.S.M.A.	Royal Society of Marine Artists
S.S.	Steam Ship
U.S.	United States
*	Denotes paintings illustrated

1946 1 HARBOUR SCENE
Painted in the Dutch manner
Oil on panel, 11 x 14 ins.
In possession of the artist

1947 2 DRY DOCK
Stern view of a large ship in Dry Dock
Water colour, 15 x 20 ins.

3 ON THE JETTY
Yachtsmen on a jetty with vessels at sea
Water colour, 15 x 20 ins.

1948 4 HAULED OUT
A Yacht on the slips at Birdham
Water colour, 15 x 20 ins.

5 TIMBER POND AT LITTLEHAMPTON
View across the River Arun
Canvas, 12 x 16 ins.
Exhib. R.S.M.A.

6 BERTHED
Canvas, 20 x 30 ins.
Exhib. R.S.M.A.

7 SALUTE TO HIS MAJESTY
A Royal Yacht passing a warship *c.* 1665
Water colour, 20 x 24 ins.

1949 8 *SHIP ASHORE
Canvas, 20 x 24 ins.
Exhib. R.O.I.

9 AT LEIGH
Water colour, 15 x 20 ins.
Exhib. R.S.M.A.

10 EDINBURGH CASTLE
A military band on the parade ground
Canvas, 20 x 30 ins.

11 UNLOADING
A Thames barge discharging cargo into a cart
Canvas, 20 x 30 ins.
Exhib. R.S.M.A.
In the possession of Hon. Ewen E. Montagu, C.B.E., Q.C.

1950 12 *MALDON, ESSEX
A view of the town from the waterside
Canvas, 40 x 50 ins.
Exhib. R.O.I.

13 LITTLEHAMPTON
View from the west side of the River Arun
Canvas, 24 x 30 ins.

14 SAILING MATCH
Canvas, 20 x 30 ins.

15 BEFORE THE LAUNCH
A ship of 1665 on the ways with a crowd of onlookers
Water colour, 20 x 30 ins.
Exhib. R.I.

16 PUTNEY
Boats on the towpath
Canvas, 22 x 30 ins.
Exhib. R.B.A. (Winter exhibition 1950, No. 447)

17 THE 'TABOR'
A ship of the Moss Hutchinson Line
Canvas, 22 x 30 ins.

1951 18 CHELSEA REACH
Houseboats on the foreshore
Canvas, 16 x 20 ins.
In possession of the artist

19 RETURN TRIP
A passenger steamer being boarded
Water colour, 18 x 22 ins.
Exhib. R.I.

20 THE LANDING
Water colour, 15 x 20 ins.
Exhib. R.I.

21 FITTING OUT
A ship in a yard
Canvas, 24 x 30 ins.

1952 22 RICHMOND, SURREY
View of the town and foreshore from below the bridge
Canvas, 40 x 50 ins.
Exhib. R.O.I.

23 NAVAL VESSEL OFF CARACAS
Canvas, 20 x 30 ins.

24 S.Y. 'MOUETTE'
The Yacht in a N.E. gale in the Kattegat
Canvas, 20 x 30 ins.
In the possession of Dr. Le Marquand

25 THE COLCHESTER ROAD
Canvas, 24 x 30 ins.
Exhib. R.B.A. (Winter exhibition 1952, No. 240)

26 EAST COAST
Exhib. R.B.A. (Winter exhibition 1952, No. 236)

1953 27 *THE 'GOTHIC'
H.M. The Queen arriving at Sydney Harbour in the *Gothic* for the start of the 1953 Commonwealth Tour. The *Gothic* dressed over-all and flying the Royal Standard with Sydney Bridge in the background.
Canvas, 30 x 40 ins.
In the National Maritime Museum, Greenwich

28 ROYAL PRECEDENT
H.R.H. Prince Philip over Buckingham Palace in a Helicopter.
Canvas, 28 x 36 ins.
In the possession of H.R.H. The Duke of Edinburgh

29 H.M.S. 'GREENOCK'
Canvas, 20 x 30 ins.

30 CROSS CHANNEL
A Yacht and a cross-channel steamer passing in the English Channel.
Canvas, 30 x 50 ins.
Exhib. R.S.M.A.

31 AN INVESTITURE
An investiture by H.M. The Queen on board the Royal Yacht *Britannia* in Gibraltar Harbour, May 1953.
Canvas, 24 x 48 ins.

1954 32 RIDING SCHOOL
In Richmond Park, Surrey
Water colour, 11 x 15 ins.

33 HUNGERFORD BRIDGE
From above showing the River Thames and the South Bank
Canvas, 30 x 50 ins.
In possession of the artist

34 DARTMOUTH
Water colour, 18 x 24 ins.

35 HOPE COVE
Water colour, 11 x 15 ins.

36 BEESANDS
Water colour, 11 x 15 ins.
Exhib. R.I.

37 THE MAWDDACH ESTUARY
Canvas, 28 x 36 ins.

38 *A ROYAL OCCASION
A Fleet of 18th Century Warships
Canvas, 30 x 50 ins.

39 H.M.S. 'VANGUARD'
Canvas, 24 x 36 ins.
In the possession of Captain J. S. S. Litchfield, O.B.E., R.N.

40 *THE RETURN FROM THE 1953 COMMONWEALTH TOUR
The Royal Yacht *Britannia* in the Thames off the Tower of London with escorting vessels
Canvas, 26 x 52 ins.
In the possession of H.M. The Queen

41 BRITISH RAIL FERRY STEAMER 'ST. DAVID'
Gouache, 22 x 30 ins.

42 *THE TANKER 'TINA ONASSIS'
Canvas, 21 x 40 ins.
In possession of Olympic Maritime

1955 43 PASSING OF THE ROYAL YACHT 'VICTORIA & ALBERT' (1899-1953)
The partially dismantled *Victoria & Albert* being towed away by Tugs, with the new Royal Yacht *Britannia,* with her signal flags hoisted, about to pass. Watchers from an adjacent yard in the left-hand corner.
Canvas, 25 x 50 ins.
In the National Maritime Museum, Greenwich

44 H.R.H. PRINCESS MARGARET AT JAMAICA
The Royal Yacht *Britannia* in the background
Canvas, 30 x 40 ins.

45 QUEEN ELIZABETH THE FIRST AT TILBURY, 1588
Canvas, 28 x 36 ins.

46 THE LAST VOYAGE OF THE 'CUTTY SARK'
The famous Clipper being towed into the specially prepared dry dock at Greenwich – her final resting place, 10th December, 1954
Canvas, 28 x 36 ins.
In the National Maritime Museum, Greenwich

47 GREENWICH
Canvas, 28 x 36 ins.

48 LIVERPOOL
From the water front
Canvas, 28 x 36 ins.

49. LINCOLN'S INN FIELDS, LONDON
Water colour, 15 x 20 ins.
Exhib. R.I.

1956 50 *MENAI BRIDGE
Viewed from the Anglesey side
Canvas, 28 x 36 ins.

51 *OLD ST. PAUL'S
Viewed from the north-east
Canvas, 28 x 26 ins.

52 OLD ST. PAUL'S
Interior view
Canvas, 28 x 36 ins.

53 TO A NEW WORLD
The *Mayflower* leaving Plymouth with the 'Plymouth Brethren' in 1620
Canvas, 40 x 50 ins.

54 H.M.S. 'HOOD'
Canvas, 25 x 40 ins.
In an American private collection

55 HEAVY WEATHER
Canvas, 28 x 36 ins.

56 THE 'DUKE OF LANCASTER'
The British Railways Ferry Steamer
Canvas, 22 x 40 ins.
In the possession of British Rail

1957 57 LAUNCHING OF THE 'AL-MALIK-SAUD-AL-AWAL'
Canvas, 30 x 40 ins.
In the possession of Olympic Maritime

59 FLENSING A WHALE ON A WHALING SHIP
Canvas, 30 x 40 ins.
In the possession of Olympic Maritime

60 THE 'OLYMPIC SPLENDOUR' & 'OLYMPIC THUNDER'
Canvas, 40 x 50 ins.
In the possession of Olympic Maritime

61 'GREEK TRIREME'
Canvas, 28 x 36 ins.
In the possession of Olympic Maritime

62 CAPTURE OF CAPE BRETON, NOVA SCOTIA, CANADA, 1763
Canvas, 25 x 40 ins.

63 *GREENOCK, 1830
Looking down from a hillside
Canvas, 72 x 60 ins.
In the possession of British & Commonwealth Shipping Co., Ltd.

64 TOWPATH, BARNES
Looking towards Chiswick Church
Canvas, 20 x 30 ins.
Exhib. R.B.A.
In the possession of the artist

65 EYNESFORD
Canvas, 20 x 24 ins.
Exhib. R.B.A.

66 TUG AGROUND AT BARNES
Canvas, 24 x 30 ins.
Exhib. R.B.A.

67 H.M.S. 'DUCHESS' ESCORTING THE ROYAL YACHT 'BRITANNIA'
Canvas, 24 x 36 ins.
In possession of Sir John Thorneycroft, C.B.E.

68 SQUALLY WEATHER
A barge in a rain storm
In possession of the artist

69 THE BATTLESHIP H.M.S. 'KING GEORGE V'
Her war service included action in the Pacific during her strike at the Sakishima Group of Islands, whilst the Americans landed on nearby Okinawa.
Canvas, 30 x 50 ins.

1958 70 *THE 'ARGYLLSHIRE'
Canvas, 24 x 36 ins.

71 M.S. 'CLAN McIVER'
Canvas, 24 x 36 ins.
In possession of the Clan Line Steamers Ltd., London.

72 THE FIGHT BETWEEN THE 'CLAN MACINTOSH' AND THE GERMAN RAIDER 'MOEWE'
Canvas, 24 x 36 ins.
In possession of the Clan Line Steamers Ltd., London.

73 THE 'CLAN SINCLAIR' OFF TABLE MOUNTAIN, CAPE TOWN
Canvas, 24 x 36 ins.
In possession of the Clan Line Steamers Ltd., London.

74 THE 'CLAN FORBES' IN THE INDIAN OCEAN
Canvas, 24 x 36 ins.
In possession of the Clan Line Steamers Ltd., London.

75 THE 'BARON GARLOCK'
Canvas, 30 x 40 ins.

76 *THE 'PENDENNIS CASTLE' & THE 'CLAN MALCOLM' OFF DURBAN
Canvas, 30 x 56 ins.
In possession of the Union Castle Mail Steamship Co., Ltd.

77 *THE 'CLAN SUTHERLAND'
At Galle, the seaport of Ceylon
Canvas, 24 x 36 ins.
In possession of the Clan Line Steamers Ltd., London.

78 *THE 'CLAN OGILVIE'
Canvas, 24 x 36 ins.
In possession of the Clan Line Steamers Ltd., London.

1959 79 LOW WATER, CHISWICK
Canvas, 20 x 24 ins.
Exhib. R.B.A. (Winter 1959, No. 270)

80 MIDLAND BRIDGE
Canvas, 20 x 24 ins.
Exhib. R.B.A. (Winter 1959, No. 273)

81 AN OBSERVATION POST OF THE 1st KING'S DRAGOON GUARDS NEAR CASSINO, ITALY, 1944
Canvas, 30 x 45 ins.
In the possession of the 1st Queen's Dragoon Guards

82 THE 1st KING'S DRAGOON GUARDS IN THE BREAK OUT FROM TOBRUK
Canvas, 30 x 45 ins.
In the possession of the 1st Queen's Dragoon Guards

1960 83 H.R.H. PRINCE PHILIP ON A JACKSTAY FROM H.M.S. 'ALBION' TO THE ROYAL YACHT 'BRITANNIA'
Canvas, 24 x 36 ins.
In the possession of H.R.H. The Duke of Edinburgh

84 *THE BATTLE OF JUTLAND (25th April, 1916)
Canvas, 40 x 60 ins.
In the possession of Cayzer Irvine & Co., Ltd.

85 *PORTRAIT OF H.M. QUEEN ELIZABETH THE QUEEN MOTHER
Painted for the Black Watch (Royal Highland Regiment) of Canada
Canvas, 30 x 25 ins.

86 PORTRAIT OF LORD LUGARD – FIRST GOVERNOR OF NIGERIA
Canvas, 40 x 30 ins.

87 *THE TROOP SHIP 'OXFORDSHIRE'
Canvas, 36 x 54 ins.
In the possession of the Parker Gallery, London

88 *THE 'ORIANA'
Canvas, 24 x 36 ins.

89 THE 'TRANSVAAL CASTLE'
With Table Mountain in the background
Canvas, 30 x 50 ins.
In the possession of the Union Castle Mail Steamship Co., Ltd.

1961 90 FRENCHMANS COVE
Canvas, 20 x 50 ins.

91 THE 'SERENIA'
Shell Petrol Tanker
Canvas, 24 x 36 ins.

92 THE ROYAL HAMPSHIRE REGIMENT ON THE RAPIDO RIVER
Canvas, 24 x 36 ins.

93 THE ASSAULT LANDING OF THE 1st BATTALION THE ROYAL HAMPSHIRE REGIMENT AT LE HAMEL, NORMANDY (6th June, 1944)
A regimental memorial painting
Canvas, 24 x 36 ins.
Repr. As a coloured card
In the possession of the Royal Hampshire Regiment

94 GROVE HOUSE, WALSHAM-LE-WILLOWS, NEAR BURY ST. EDMUNDS
Canvas, 18 x 24 ins.

95 WALSHAM-LE-WILLOWS
View of the village
Canvas, 18 x 24 ins.

96 'D' DAY OVER THE ENGLISH CHANNEL, (4th June, 1944)
Planes towing Gliders
Canvas, 48 x 84 ins.
In possession of the 38th Group Headquarters, Odiham

96a THE 2nd/4th BATTALION THE HAMPSHIRE REGIMENT APPROACHING THE PIOPPETA RIVER ON THE 13th MAY 1944 DURING THE SECOND BATTLE FOR CASINO, SOUTHERN ITALY
Canvas, 30 x 40 ins.
In the possession of the Royal Hampshire Regiment

97 PORT ANTONIO, JAMAICA
A view across the water
Canvas, 28 x 40 ins.

98 MAN AND A DONKEY – JAMAICA
One of some 20 sketches in oil put together for an exhibition while the artist was in Jamaica
Oil on panel, 12 x 18 ins.

1962 99 *THE CLIPPER SHIP 'MIDDLESEX'
Canvas, 24 x 36 ins.

100 YACHT RACE
Canvas, 30 x 40 ins.

101 *COLUMBUS LANDING (12th October, 1492)
Canvas, 26 x 40 ins.
Formerly in the possession of the late K. Helweg Larsen

102 THE CHIRRIPO
Canvas, 20 x 30 ins.

1963 103 S.S. 'RINFORM'
Canvas, 24 x 36 ins.

104 PRESENTATION OF NEW COLOURS TO THE 1st BATTALION THE ROYAL HAMPSHIRE REGIMENT BY THE EARL MOUNTBATTEN OF BURMA, K.G.
At Münster, West Germany, on Minden Day, 1st August, 1963
Canvas, 22 x 40 ins.
In the possession of The Royal Hampshire Regiment

1964 105 THE CLIPPER 'NIOBE'
1469 tons
Canvas, 30 x 40 ins.

106 *H.M. CUTTER 'ACTIVE'
Canvas, 28 x 36 ins.

107 U.S. CLIPPER 'EASTERN MONARCH'
Canvas, 30 x 40 ins.

108 THE CLIPPER 'SURPRISE'
Canvas, 28 x 30 ins.
In the possession of Mr. G. D. Kemp

1965 109 *THE GREAT TEA RACE BETWEEN 'ARIEL' & 'TAEPING', 1866

Both these Clippers were built by Robert Steele & Co., at Greenock. Steele's ships were celebrated for their beauty and superb craftsmanship. The figureheads, the gingerbread work and deck fittings of selected teak, with brass inlay being very notable. *Ariel* was launched 29th June, 1865 and *Taeping* 24th December, 1863. Ariel was slightly the larger vessel having a registered tonnage of 852, her length 195 ft., whereas *Taeping* was 767 tons and 183 ft. in length. In May 1866 the most enthralling of all the tea races started from the Pagoda anchorage in the Min River and ended inside the London Dock Gates. Eleven tea clippers took part and *Ariel* was the favourite, largely due to being commanded by Captain John Kaye, probably the most experienced Master in the China trade. The struggle began before the ships hove up their anchors; it began in the offices of the ship's Agents and in the Hongs of the Chinese merchants; fortunes in money depending upon the winner. The favourite for the race got the first chests and was therefore the first to complete loading. Consequently the ships did not start at the same time, in fact they left days apart. In a race of 100 days across three-quarters of the globe, every hour was of vital importance. Each of the ships carried a picked crew, generally about thirty. Both ships left the Min River on May 30. At the Cape *Ariel* was only twelve hours ahead of *Taeping,* and in the passage up the Atlantic five ships got closer and closer to each other. On the equator *Taeping, Fiery Cross* and *Ariel* all crossed the line on 4th August. A month later, *Ariel* and *Taeping* were sailing up the English Channel. One may imagine the excitement both aboard the two ships and ashore when the news they were racing so close spread. From every headland the report of their positions was rushed to the nearest Post Office and the owners and agents in London soon learnt that the two vessels were neck and neck. In the Downs after ninety days at sea there was but ten minutes difference between the two, with *Ariel* having a slight edge. But the race was not finished until the boxes of tea were hurled ashore in the London Dock, and it was very unfortunate for *Ariel* that *Taeping's* tug proved faster and in the end she docked twenty minutes ahead of her sister ship. Unknown to both captains the owners had agreed privately to divide the premium claimed for the ship in dock. After such a magnificent exhibition of racing seamanship it was no consolation to divide the stakes, and all shipping people agreed that the race should have finished when the leading ship took aboard her pilot.

Canvas, 40 x 60 ins.

In the possession of John Wallrock, Esq.

110 THE U.S. CLIPPER 'CITY OF MOBILE'

Canvas, 30 x 40 ins.

111 A NEW DAY – A TRAWLER AT DAWN

Canvas, 20 x 30 ins.

112 *THE EAST INDIAMAN 'EARL OF BALCARRES'

Canvas, 30 x 40 ins.

113 THE YACHTS 'HENRIETTA', 'VESTA' & 'FLEETWING' IN THE ATLANTIC YACHT RACE OF 1864

Canvas, 30 x 40 ins.

In the possession of Dr. Beppé Croce

114 CHINA TEA CLIPPER 'THERMOPYLAE'

See also Cat. No. 139 for a second version of this Clipper and Cat. No. 156.

Canvas, 35 x 39 ins.

Auct. Christie's, 6th October, 1972 (28)

Originally in a Canadian collection (1965)

1966 115 *H.R.H. PRINCE OF WALES LEAVING PLYMOUTH FOR NORTH AMERICA, 1860 ABOARD H.M.S. HERO

Ships of the Line fully dressed with yard arms lined with sailors giving his Royal Highness a Royal send-off, around are boats crowded with waving folk. This picture was painted for Liberty's of Regent Street, London, showing the two 'Wooden Walls' *H.M.S's Hindustan & Impregnable* from whose timbers the large Liberty Shop in Marlborough Street was built.

In the possession of Liberty, & Co. Ltd., London

116 *MR. PEPYS' NAVY

The Fleet assembled in the Downs in May, 1660 preparatory to sailing to bring home Charles II from the Netherlands.

Canvas, 48 x 96 ins.

Exhib. R.S.M.A.

In the possession of Mr. J. Jervis

117 THE 'WORTHING BELLE' LOADING PASSENGERS AT LITTLEHAMPTON

Canvas, 30 x 40 ins.

Exhib. R.S.M.A.

In the possession of the Artist

118 ARRIVAL AT NASSAU OF H.M. THE QUEEN IN THE ROYAL YACHT 'BRITANNIA', 1966

Canvas, 25 x 42 ins.

119 HER MAJESTY QUEEN ELIZABETH II TAKING THE SALUTE AT NASSAU IN THE BAHAMAS, 1966

Oil, 25 x 42 ins.

120 M.S. 'SIDONIA'

This vessel belonged to the Anchor Line

Canvas, 24 x 36 ins.

121 THE CLIPPER 'ADELAIDE'

Canvas, 30 x 40 ins.

122 *THE 'CUTTY SARK'

They mark our passage as a race of men,
Earth will not see such ships as those agen.
John Masefield – 'Ships'

The *Cutty Sark* (her name comes from Robert Burns' poem 'Tam o'Shanter' and the words mean short chemise or shift) was probably the most famous of all the clippers, a composite ship of 962.97 tons gross, 921.39 net registered tons, and with an under deck tonnage of 892 tons. She was built at Dumbarton by Scott and Linton for London shipowner John Willis, and was launched on 22nd November, 1869 and registered as belonging to the Port of London. Captain John Willis had his office in Leadenhall Street, but although an old sea captain, he never commanded the *Cutty Sark,* whose first Master was Captain George Moodie. The designer of the *Cutty Sark,* Hercules Linton, was taken by Willis to see his favourite ship, the *Tweed,* in dry dock; but although she may have influenced the young designer to some extent, the stern of the *Cutty Sark,* with its beautifully clean run, was entirely Linton's own work. She made many fast runs from Shanghai with tea for London in the region of 109 days. In 1872 she raced with the *Thermopylae* from Shanghai, and in this race she lost her rudder. Although it took 5 days to make and fit a jury rudder replacement, in spite

of this setback the *Cutty Sark* reached the Downs less than a week behind her rival. It was generally thought that had the *Cutty Sark* not lost her rudder, she would have been the winner of this classic race. From 1870 to 1877 she was engaged in the China tea trade, but really made her fame between 1883 and 1895 in the Australian wool run, many of her passages taking less than 80 days. In 1895 she was sold to the Portuguese and renamed the *Ferreira,* trading between Portugal and the colonies for many years, unremembered by Britain, until in 1922 she was bought back by Captain Wilfred Dowman of Falmouth, where he re-rigged her and fitted her out as a training ship for boys of the Royal and Merchant Navies. Remaining in Falmouth until he died shortly before the War, she was given by his widow in 1938 to the Incorporated Thames Nautical Training College at Greenhithe, where she joined H.M.S. *Worcester.* When, after the War, the Nautical Training College acquired a newer, larger ship to replace the old *Worcester,* they no longer required the *Cutty Sark* for training. At this stage, a Society was formed to preserve and exhibit the fully re-rigged ship at Greenwich, close by the Royal Naval College, and she was berthed in a special dock built there to contain her on 10th December, 1954, and opened to the public by H.M. The Queen on 25th June, 1957 as a national memorial to the glorious days of sail. The original Lloyd's Register survey report on the *Cutty Sark,* dated 7th January 1870, and signed by Alexander Linton, father to Hercules, has been presented to the Cutty Sark Society, and placed with the National Maritime Museum.
Canvas, 30 x 40 ins.
In the possession of Mr. J. Lyman

1967 123 OUT ON THE EBB
A Brigantine towing out from Littlehampton Harbour
Canvas, 26 x 30 ins.
Auct. Messenger, May & Baverstock, Godalming, 22nd October, 1969 (53)

124 THREE ROYAL NAVY SHIPS AND THE R.N.V.R. YACHT
Canvas, 30 x 45 ins.
Presented by the Artist to the Royal Naval Volunteer Club, London

125 THE UNITED STATES FRIGATE 'CONSTITUTION'
Designed by Joshua Hempries and built by George Claighorne at the Hartt Shipyard in Boston. This Frigate, one of America's first ships of war, was launched on 21st October, 1797, commissioned into the Navy, putting to sea in July 1798. She first went into action in the Napoleonic wars and was active against French Privateers in 1799. In 1803 she was flagship of the Mediterranean fleet against the Barbary Corsairs. In the war of 1812, she captured the *Guerriere* off St. Lawrence, was in action against the *Java* 29th December, 1812 off the coast of Brazil. Captured two British Sloops, *Cyane* and *Levant,* off Cape Verde in July, 1815. She was rebuilt several times, then during 1844-46 made an 18-month tour of the world under Captain Percival. Saw service until 1855, and carried goods to the Paris Exhibition of 1877 eighty years after she was launched. In 1906 rebuilt as a Naval Museum, in 1931 she made a tour of some twenty major American ports, and since 1934 has been at Boston.
Canvas, 28 x 36 ins.

126 THE MARTYRDOM OF ST. CLEMENT
Fishermen discovering his body
Canvas, 20 x 24 ins.

127 THE YACHT 'MARABOU'
Canvas, 20 x 30 ins.
In the possession of the Coastal Forces Sailing Club

128 *THE U.S. CLIPPER 'YOUNG AMERICA'
Canvas, 28 x 40 ins.

129 THE U.S. CLIPPER 'CHAMPION OF THE SEAS'
Canvas, 28 x 36 ins.
In the possession of Senator G. McGovern, U.S.A.

130 SIR JAMES HUNT
Portrait painted for Grey College, Durham
Canvas

131 THE U.S. CLIPPER 'APOLLO'
Canvas, 28 x 40 ins.

1968 132 THE LAUNCH
A small fishing boat launching off a beach
Canvas, 28 x 36 ins.
In the possession of Mr. J. Lyman

133 H.M.S. 'NEWCASTLE'
Canvas, 30 x 50 ins.

134 *U.S. CLIPPER 'ARCHER'
Canvas, 28 x 40 ins.

135 U.S. CLIPPER 'CHALLENGE'
Canvas, 30 x 40 ins.

136 U.S. CLIPPER 'WILD PIDGEON'
Canvas, 24 x 36 ins.

137 *U.S. CLIPPER 'STARLIGHT'
Canvas, 28 x 40 ins.

138 *U.S. CLIPPER 'PRIMA DONNA'
Canvas, 25 x 40 ins.

139 *THE 'THERMOPYLAE'

The Ships that raced the wool,
The grain, the jute, the tea,
'Titania' beautiful,
and proud 'Thermopylae'

The *Thermopylae* (948 tons), was built in 1868 by Walter Hood of Aberdeen for George Thompson, who owned the Aberdeen White Star line, and was launched 19th August, 1868. She was the great rival to the *Cutty Sark*, and made one of the fastest passages of all the tea clippers – leaving Foochow on 3rd July, 1870, docking in England in 91 days. Despite other claims she was considered to be the fastest ship of her size ever built, and she certainly held a number of unbroken records. She was engaged in the tea trade between 1868 and 1882; and thereafter in the Australian wool trade until 1890, when she was sold to a Mr. Retford of Montreal, for whom she carried rice from Rangoon to Vancouver. She was eventually purchased by the Portuguese Government for use as a training ship and re-*Pedro Nunes.* She had an honourable ending, when on 13th October, 1907, she was towed out of the Tagus to sea by two warships and torpedoed. In her heyday she was affectionately known as the fast 'Green Clipper' because of the colour of her hull.
(See also Cat. No. 114 & 156)
Canvas, 28 x 30 ins.

140 THE YACHT 'ROMANCE'
Shown in Caribbean waters
Canvas, 16 x 20 ins.

141 THE TUGS 'FIERY CROSS' & 'AYTON CROSS' IN THE RIVER TEES
Canvas, 28 x 56 ins.
In the possession of the Tees Towing Co., Ltd.

142 GROUP OF U.S. NAVAL COMMANDS OF MR. CROALE
Canvas, 40 x 70 ins.
In the possession of Mr. M. Croale

143 *THE CONFEDERATE CRUISER 'ALABAMA' FORCING THE AMERICAN CLIPPER 'WINGED RACER' TO HEAVE TO, 19th October, 1863
Canvas, 36 x 60 ins.

144 A 'J' CLASS YACHT OFF COWES
Canvas, 40 x 70 ins.

145 NORWEGIAN HAVEN
Fishing Trawlers in a Fjord
Canvas, 20 x 30 ins.

146 SHIP OFF LITTLEHAMPTON PICKING UP A PILOT
Canvas, 29 x 30 ins.

1969 147 THE PICNIC
A romantic landscape
Canvas, 36 x 48 ins.
In the possession of the Artist

148 *CHARLES DICKENS LEAVING LIVERPOOL IN THE PACKET 'GEORGE WASHINGTON' IN 1842
Canvas, 40 x 60 ins.

149 CHARLES DICKENS LEAVING NEW YORK
He made the return to England in the same Packet, 7th June 1842
Canvas, 40 x 60 ins.

150 BAR. 29 AND STILL FALLING
Fishing craft in worsening weather
Canvas, 20 x 24 ins.

151 *THE OPIUM CLIPPER 'FALCON'
Canvas, 28 x 36 ins.

152 PROFESSOR ERIC BIRLEY
Portrait painted for Hatfield College, Durham
Canvas

1970 153 *THE YACHT 'MYSTIC' OFF DIAMOND ROCK, HAWAII
Canvas, 30 x 40 ins.
In the possession of Mr. Marvyn Carton

154 THE CONFEDERATE CRUISER 'ALABAMA' OFF CAPETOWN INTERCEPTING THE U.S. CLIPPER 'SEA BRIDE'
Canvas, 30 x 48 ins.
Formerly in the possession of the late Dr. H. Luttig

155 *THE 'HERZOGIN CECILE'
Canvas, 30 x 40 ins.

156 *THE 'NORMAN COURT'
The *Norman Court* was a tea clipper, composite built in 1869 by J. & A. Inglis for the famous Baring Brothers. She had a registered tonnage of 855 tons, and while being extremely lofty she was handy to a degree. Named after one of the Baring family's homes, in Hampshire, she had a figurehead carved to the likeness of one of the family beauties. She was handsomely fitted with a solid brass rail round her bulwarks and had the builder kept strictly to the design that Rennie had provided for the moulding of the iron frames she might have been an even greater masterpiece. Her maiden voyage under the Master, Captain Sherman, was made in 105 days to Hong Kong. She was engaged in the tea trade with China, making many fast runs. In 1870 in a race with *Thermopylae,* she actually completed the passage from Foochow to Deal in one day less than the famous Green Clipper which was reputed to be capable of seven knots in 'an air which would not extinguish a candle'.
Canvas, 28 x 40 ins.

157 *THE CLIPPER 'SOUTH AUSTRALIAN'
Built 1868 of 1078 tons.
Canvas, 30 x 45 ins.

158 *THE CLIPPERS 'METEOR', 'GAMECOCK' & 'TELEGRAPH' AT GOLDEN GATE

In calm magnificence the sun declined
and left a paradise of cloud behind

Canvas, 30 x 46ins.

159 HOME AT LAST
Canvas, 20 x 30 ins.

160 U.S. CLIPPER 'DASHING WAVE'

Strong and free, strong and free
The floodgates are open, away to the sea

Canvas, 30 x 40 ins.
Auct. Christie's, 6th October, 1972 (26)

161 THE STUART ROYAL YACHT 'MARY'
Off Greenwich with the old Palace in the background
Canvas, 40 x 60 ins.
In the possession of Dr. Beppé Croce

162 *THE ROYAL YACHT 'BRITANNIA' RACING IN THE SOLENT
Oil, 40 x 60 ins.
In the possession of Dr. Beppé Croce

1971 163 *THE 'MAYFLOWER' & 'SPEEDWELL'
The *Mayflower* and *Speedwell* in Dartmouth Harbour 14th August 1620, where the *Speedwell* underwent repairs during their voyage from Southampton to Plymouth before sailing to America with the Pilgrim Fathers.
Canvas, 42 x 84 ins.
In the possession of the Pilgrim Society, Plymouth, Massachusetts

164 *JEANNETTE

Based on an incident towards the close of the Battle of Trafalgar, 1805, when among 250 survivors rescued by British seamen from the French warship *Achille* was a young Frenchwoman who had stowed away to be with her husband, with whom she was later to be reunited. The rescue operation by a boat from H.M.S. *Pickle* was a dangerous one, for the *Achille* had caught fire and her guns were going off one by one until about 5 p.m., when the flames reached her magazine and she blew up. This event has been described as 'sounding the last note of the rout in Trafalgar's Bay'. Apart from its unique maritime subject, the painting is noteworthy in that it commanded the highest price at the exhibition, being sold at five thousand guineas.

Canvas, 40 x 60 ins.

Exhib. R.M.S.A. (Jubilee exhibition) at the London Guildhall, October-November, 1970

In the possession of Mr. Garfield Weston

165 *BARQUE TOWING OUT OF LITTLEHAMPTON HARBOUR

I'm afloat – I'm afloat – on the fierce rolling tide;
The ocean's my home! and my Bark is my bride

Here is a scene from everyday life in the nineteenth century, a fussy paddle-propelled tugboat belching black smoke towing out a merchant vessel. Onlookers line the jetty.

Canvas, 30 x 45 ins.

Exhib. Painted for the King Edward VII Hospital exhibition.

166 *U.S. CLIPPER 'RAVEN' LEAVING FALMOUTH

Canvas, 30 x 45 ins.

167 *THE U.S. CLIPPER 'RINGLEADER' AT FOOCHOW

Canvas, 30 x 45 ins.

168 THE 'JOHN LOCKETT'

Canvas, 20 x 30 ins.

In the possession of Mr. G. D. Lockett

169 THE 'LAHORE'

Canvas, 20 x 30 ins.

In the possession of Mr. G. D. Lockett

170 IN PORT FOR CHRISTMAS

Fishermen coming ashore and meeting their families

Canvas, 20 x 30 ins.

171 U.S. CLIPPER 'MALAY' AT FOOCHOW

Canvas, 30 x 45 ins.

172 U.S. CLIPPER 'GOLDEN WEST'

Canvas, 30 x 40 ins.

173 *U.S. CLIPPER 'FLYING EAGLE'

Canvas, 30 x 40 ins.

174 *U.S. CLIPPER 'GOLDEN EAGLE'

Canvas, 30 x 40 ins.

1972 175 *THE 'BOUNTY' AT MATAVIA BAY, TAHITI, 1789

Captain Bligh loading breadfruit

Canvas, 25 x 40 ins.

176 *SHIPWRECK

Ye gentlemen of England
That live at home at ease
Ah! Little do you think upon
The Dangers of the seas

A ship dismasted on a stormy sea.
Canvas, 27 x 40 ins.

177 *CAPTAIN ARTHUR PHILIPS LANDING AT SYDNEY COVE, AUSTRALIA, 1788
Canvas, 25 x 40 ins.
In a private Australian collection

178 THE 'OXFORD'
The Blackball Packet leaving Liverpool with emigrants. She was built in 1836 by Webb & Allen of New York (of 752 tons). Made many consistently good passages and, like most of the early lines, was well kept and a credit to her owners. She is seen here backing into the stream, a manoeuvre possible only when handled by a skilled Master and crew.
Exhib. The Parker Gallery, London (April 1973)
Canvas, 40 x 60 ins.

179 *THE 'JOHN GILPIN' AT BOSTON
In the days of the sailing ships, Boston was perhaps the busiest port of America and here we see the *John Gilpin* arriving and about to drop anchor. The jetty crowded with expectant relations from the old country perhaps!
Canvas, 40 x 60 ins.

180 *R.N.V.R. TRAWLER OFF PORTSMOUTH (World War II)
Painted to commemorate the 25th anniversary of the Scottish R.N.V.R. and unveiled on that occasion by H.R.H. Prince Philip in the *Carrick,* where it now hangs.
Canvas, 30 x 45 ins.

181 U.S. CLIPPER 'AMERICAN REPORTER'
Canvas, 30 x 45 ins.

182 THE YACHT 'SOLIMAR' IN THE CARIBBEAN
Canvas, 33 x 40 ins.
Painted for the owner Mr. G. B. Cole

183 U.S. CLIPPER SOVEREIGN OF THE SEAS
Built by Donald McKay in 1832, and of 2421 American register tons, she was at that time one of the largest if not actually the largest clipper ship afloat. Her crew numbered 105 all told. She had a number of very fast runs across the Atlantic and in 1853 she actually beat the Cunard Steamship *Canada* en route to Liverpool, a performance of the highest order.
Oil on board, 20 x 24 ins.

184 *THE CLIPPER 'RED JACKET'

A wet sheet and a flowing sea,
A wind that follows fast
And fills the white and rustling sail
And bends the gallant mast.

The *Red Jacket* was built by Thomas of Maine in 1853 of oak and copper fastened. With her registered tonnage of 2460, there were few larger clippers, and she was also fast, making

one of the shortest passages to Liverpool from Maine, sailing the 2,020 miles in 13 days and 1 hour. On her arrival in Liverpool she was immediately chartered by the White Star Line and put into the Australian run, making a number of record passages under Captain S. Reed. She made the Australian run in 69 days. Her racing strained her badly and in the 1870s she was condemned.
Canvas, 30 x 40 ins.

185 THE CLIPPER 'FLYING CLOUD'
The *Flying Cloud* was built in East Boston in 1851, in an endeavour to speed up communications between New York and San Francisco, because of the Gold Rush of 1851. She was 208 feet long, 40 ft. 8 ins. broad and 21 ft. 6 ins. deep, with a tonnage of 1728, old American tons.
Oil on board, 20 x 24 ins.

186 CUTTY SARK
(See Catalogue No. 122)
Oil on board, 20 x 24 ins.

187 POSEIDON & ODYSSEUS
The God attempting the destruction of Odysseus.
Canvas, 33 x 45 ins.

188 ON DUTY
The Royal National Mission to Deep Sea Fishermen at Newlyn Quay, Cornwall
Canvas, 20 x 30 ins.

189 CRAMPS SHIPYARD AT PHILADELPHIA
At end of the last century
Canvas, 20 x 30 ins.
In the possession of Mr. W. Cramp Scheetz, Junior

190 THE 'COURIER'
Canvas, 20 x 30 ins.
In the possession of Mr. G. D. Lockett

191 *UNITED STATES FLEET RETURNING TO NEW YORK AFTER THE SPANISH -AMERICAN WAR, 1898 – THE 'BROOKLYN' & 'INDIANA'
Canvas, 24 x 36 ins.
In the possession of Mr. W. Cramp Scheetz, Junior

192 THE 'J. T. NORTH'
Canvas, 20 x 30 ins.
In the possession of Mr. G. Lockett

193 *U.S. CLIPPER 'OCEAN ROVER'
Oil, 24 x 36 ins.

1973 194 WESTBROOK HOUSE, GODALMING
In the eighteenth century
Canvas, 30 x 40 ins.
In the possession of Mr. M. B. Lane

195 *U.S. CLIPPER 'ORIENTAL'
The Clipper entering the old West India Dock Gate, Limehouse
(see also Catalogue No. 203)
Canvas, 27 x 40 ins.

196 BRIG ASHORE
At a river mouth with a hilly background
Canvas, 16 x 20 ins.

197 *BRIGHTON BEACH, *c.* 1850
Two colliers beached at low tide being unloaded into the two-wheel carts of the time. It shows one of the carts being run up the beach. A dirty and laborious affair, baskets being filled and swung out to tip into the waiting cart.
Canvas, 20 x 30 ins.

198* HIGH WATER AT GRAVESEND
When coal was still the fuel for Thames tugs, the bow waves and the smoke combining with the mist created pictures which now no longer occur. The tall funnels, with their coloured bands, were a constant source of interest amongst the river traffic.
ERhib. The Parker Gallery, London (April 1973)
Canvas, 19 x 36 ins.

199 *THE CLIPPER 'STAGHOUND' OFF SANDY HOOK
With a Pilot Cutter standing by in a mist. Designed and built by Donald McKay of East Boston (1534 tons) and launched in 1850 for Sampson & Tappen of Boston East, Mass. She was the largest American merchantman at the time of her launch. Given the right conditions *Staghound* was a fast ship, although she was not a good carrier. Her interior fittings were exceptional, indicative of the pride McKay took in his creations.
Canvas, 40 x 60ins.

200 THE U.S. PACKET 'DREADNOUGHT'
Shown in a rough sea, with her keel half out of the water as seen by another ship's Captain. The *Dreadnought* was perhaps the most famous of all the packet ships which ran across the Atlantic. Built in 1853 at Newburyport, and of 1413 tons register, she accomplished a great number of fast runs from New York to Liverpool, averaging just over 14 days. Known as the 'Wild Ship of the Atlantic', due to the driving power of her Master, Captain Samuels.
Canvas, 30 x 40 ins.
Exhib. The Parker Gallery, London (April 1973)

201 *U.S. CLIPPER 'HERALD OF THE MORNING'
Rounding Cape Horn
Canvas, 30 x 45 ins.

202 THE RIVER ARUN
A small sailing vessel on the river, a farm worker with a horse on the towpath. Arundel in the background with the Castle overlooking the town.
Canvas, 18 x 13 ins.
In the possession of Mr. Graham Rees

203 U.S. CLIPPER 'ORIENTAL' AT HONG KONG
Built in 1849 by Jacob Bell for A. A. Low & Brothers of New York for the China trade. She was 1003 tons
Canvas, 30 x 45 ins.
Exhib. The Parker Gallery, London (April 1973)

204 MORGAN AT PORT ROYAL, JAMAICA
Port Royal was built on a Cay at the tip of the Palisadoes, a sand spit which curves round

what is now Kingston Harbour. Originally a collection of fishermen's huts named Cagua, and renamed Port Royal in honour of the restored Stuart Monarchy. In 1692 Port Royal was entirely engulfed when it sank below the sea after one of the worst earthquakes in history. The cemetery where Morgan lay sank under the water and nothing now remains of what was once the buccaneer's stronghold. During his early years in Jamaica, Morgan was a pure filibuster, but later proved to be a first class military commander and, as Sir Henry Morgan, was appointed Lieutenant Governor of Jamaica in 1674.
Canvas, 30 x 45 ins.
Exhib. The Parker Gallery, London (April 1973)

205 'SOOLOO' LEAVING GENOA
A typical Mediterranean trader of the last century. Built at Salem, Massachusetts (400 tons) and owned by Benjamin Silsbee. No large vessels, such as the Clippers, used the Mediterranean . Smaller traders like *Sooloo* were the most common of the merchantment of Britain, America, and other countries to call at its ports.
Canvas, 30 x 45 ins.
Exhib. Parker Gallery, London (1973)

206 *THE WHALER 'JULIAN' OF NEW BEDFORD
This specialised vessel was built at Duxbury, Massachusetts in 1828 and was of 365 tons.
Canvas, 22 x 30 ins.
Exhib. The Parker Gallery, London (1973)

207 THE 'LOCH TORRIDON' OFF SYDNEY HEAD, N.S.W., AUSTRALIA
Built by Barclay Curle at Glasgow in 1881 (2000 tons) for Aitken & Lilburne for the Australian Run. She was one of the fastest and most elegant four-mast Barques in the British Mercantile Marine. In 1912 she was sold to Russia where she survived until 1915, when she foundered near the English Channel.
Canvas, 27 x 40 ins.
Exhib. The Parker Gallery, London (1973)

208 THE 'SAVANNAH'
The first steamship to cross the Atlantic. Built in 1819 (319 tons) in New York and intended as a Packet on the New York to Le Havre run. Captain Moses Reynolds, who had considerable experience of Steamers on American rivers, persuaded a Savannah firm to buy her and convert the ship to steam. The latter was only intended to be auxiliary and was a single-cylinder engine driving paddles which could be unshipped and carried on deck. Her first passage was from New York to Savannah, where it was advertised she would sail for Liverpool. She left on 22nd May 1819, and arrived off Cork on 17th June. She had used up all her coal, although she had only been under steam for 80 hours, finishing the voyage under sail. On the return passage the engine was not used until she was inside the Savannah river. In 1820 she was sold to new owners who immediately removed the engine.
Canvas, 27 x 40 ins.
Exhib. The Parker Gallery, London (April 1973)

209 *THE U.S. CLIPPER 'STARR KING' IN COMPANY WITH THE CLIPPER 'WITCHCRAFT', 28th August 1854
The *Starr King* was built by George Jackman, Jnr., at Newburyport (1171 tons) for Baker & Morrill of Boston. The two Clippers are shown on a voyage from San Francisco to Callao.
Canvas, 30 x 45 ins.

210 THE YACHT 'HENRIETTA' & THE CLIPPER 'WILD DEER'
On Christmas Day, 1866, Gordon Bennett's *Henrietta,* leading in the first Trans-Atlantic Yacht race, hauled out from Portland and tried her paces with *Wild Deer* on her way home from China. The two vessels stayed together for a time until Bennett bore away for the Needles. *Wild Deer* was the first composite ship built by Charles Connell on the Clyde for Walter's of London. She had an elm bottom fastened with treenails and yellow metal with iron bulwarks and a 75 ft. mainyard. Under her first Master, Captain George Cobb, she made a number of fast runs, including one of 98 days from Shanghai to London. In 1866 she became the property of the Albion Shipping Company, which merged in 1882 with the famous Shaw Savill Line. Used to carry passengers and emigrants to Australia and New Zealand. On 12th January, 1883 she was wrecked on the North Rock at Cloughey, Co. Down with 200 emigrants on board.
Canvas, 27 x 40 ins.

211 *UP CHANNEL – SHORTENING SAIL
Canvas, 24 x 36 ins.
Exhib. The Parker Gallery, London (1973)

212 THE U.S. CLIPPERS 'DAVID BROWN' & 'ROMANCE OF THE SEAS' IN THE GOLDEN GATE
The *David Brown* was built by Roosevelt & Joyce of New York in 1853 (1715 tons) and *Romance of the Seas* by Donald McKay of East Boston (1782 tons) in the same year for G. Upton of Boston. These two fine Clippers were both launched in October 1853. The *David Brown* left New York, 13th December, 1853, and the *Romance of the Seas* on 16th December, both bound for San Francisco. They entered port within hours of each other on 23rd March, 1854.
Exhib. The Parker Gallery, London (1973)

213 THE ROYAL YACHTS 'BRITANNIA' & 'BLUEBOTTLE'
Here can be seen H.R.H. Prince Philip sailing on the Solent. *Bluebottle,* a Dragon class racing yacht, was a wedding gift from the Island Sailing Club to H.M. The Queen and H.R.H. The Duke of Edinburgh. *Britannia* (4000 tons) 413 ft. overall, was laid down in 1952 to take the place of the former Royal Yacht *Victoria & Albert.*
Exhib. The Parker Gallery, London (April, 1973)
Canvas, 27 x 40 ins.

214 'BRITANNIA' AND THE ROYAL YACHT 'FUBBS'
Here Charles II is seen boarding his new ship. Both were built for the King in 1682. The *Britannia* (1707 tons) was built at Chatham and measured 167 ft. 5 ins. by 47 ft. 4 ins. by 18 ft. She carried 100 guns. The *Fubbs* (148 tons) constructed by Sir Phineas Pett, measured 73 ft. 6 ins., and was the most famous of the early Royal Yachts. The name was derived from 'Fubby', the name by which Louise de Kerouaille, Duchess of Portsmouth, was known to the King.
Canvas, 27 x 40 ins.
Exhib. The Parker Gallery, London (April 1973)

215 THE 'JOHN WESLEY' AT VENICE, 1857
The American Bark *John Wesley* (520 tons) was built in 1852 at Scarsport-Maine, and is typical of the smaller merchantmen of the period. She traded between New England, with manufactured goods, and the Mediterranean and on to the West Indies where she would pick up sugar and molasses for home.
Canvas, 30 x 45 ins.
Exhib. The Parker Gallery, London (April 1973)

216 LONE PASSAGE MAKER

A thousand miles from land are we
Tossing about on the stormy sea

In a heavy sea, with a stormy sky, a lone yacht makes its way single-handed across the Atlantic.
Exhib. The Parker Gallery, London (April 1973)
Canvas, 20 x 30 ins.

217 CAPTAIN COOK WITH H.M. SHIPS 'RESOLUTION' & 'DISCOVERY' AT HAWAII IN 1778
Captain Cook in H.M.S. *Resolution* with H.M.S. *Discovery* arriving at Manui-Hawaii in November, 1778. On 18th January 1778, Cook discovered two mountainous islands, Niihau and Kahai, which he named the Sandwich Islands. The two most westerly of what is the Hawaiian Group, they were his last major discovery. On leaving the Islands he sailed north to work along the north-west coast of America, but subsequently returned to them, arriving at Maui on 26th November when many natives came out in canoes to his ship. A few days later he anchored in Kealakekua Bay, Hawaii.
Canvas, 32 x 50 ins.
Exhib. The Parker Gallery, London (1973)

218 LOADING FOR MARKET
Fishermen taking their catch to the 'carrier' vessel.
Canvas, 20 x 30 ins.

219 U.S. CLIPPER 'ORPHEUS'
Canvas, 24 x 36 ins.

220 H.M. THE QUEEN OF DENMARK'S VISIT TO GREENWICH
The Danish Royal Yacht *'Dannebrog'* in the foreground, 30th April, 1974.
Canvas, 30 x 45 ins.

1974 221 *U.S. CLIPPER 'HIGHFLYER' AT WHAMPOA
The busy port at Whampoa with *Highflyer* at anchor, Chinese junks, ferry boats and the usual scene at any busy port.
Canvas, 25 x 40 ins.

222 THE RIVER ARUN AT ARUNDEL
With Arundel Castle and the town in the background.
Canvas, 30 x 50 ins.
In the possession of the Artist

223 THE U.S. CLIPPER 'GOLDEN CITY' AT FALMOUTH
Canvas, 27 x 40 ins.

224 *THE U.S. CLIPPERS 'GAMECOCK' & 'FORMOSA'
Canvas, 27 x 40 ins.

225 U.S. CLIPPERS 'COMET' & 'DUTCHMAN'
Canvas, 24 x 36 ins.

226 THE 'JOHN GILPIN' LEAVING BOSTON
Canvas, 40 x 60 ins.

227 *RICHMOND, SURREY
View on the river.
Canvas, 24 x 42 ins.

228 THE 'J. T. CALDERON'
Canvas, 20 x 30 ins.
In the possession of Mr. G. Lockett

229 CHRISTMAS IN THE ICE PACK
Mission Steamer at Labrador.
Canvas, 20 x 30 ins.

230 *H.M. QUEEN ELIZABETH THE QUEEN MOTHER RECEIVING THE FREEDOM OF THE MUSICIANS' COMPANY, 1966
From the Master at that time – Mr. G. D. Lockett.
Canvas, 30 x 40 ins.

1975 231*THE U.S.A. NAVAL CARRIER 'VALLEY FORGE' AT HONG KONG
With a background of part of Hong Kong and the hills behind which gives an indication of the enormous size of the Carrier.
Canvas, 24 x 36 ins.
Presented to Valley Forge Military Academy by a U.S. Benefactor

232 *'GAMECOCK' & 'FORWARD HO'
Canvas, 30 x 45 ins.
Repr. Country Life, 15th May, 1975
Exhib. The Parker Gallery, London

233 *THE AMERICAN CLIPPER 'BLUE JACKET' (1790 tons)

The Sea! the sea! the open sea!
the blue, the fresh, the ever free

A powerful example of what may be called the 'Blue-seas-and-snowy-tops'ls' type of marine painting as exemplified by Leslie Wilcox – a breezy sea in which the atmospheric effect is observed in both sea and sky.
Canvas, 30 x 40 ins.

234 ALGERINE PIRATE IN THE MEDITERRANEAN
Canvas, 22 x 30 ins.

1976 235 *THE BATTLE OF BUNKER'S HILL

'Drink, John she said, 'twill' do you good, poor child you'll never bear
This working in the dismal trench
And if – God bless me! you were hurt, 'twould keep away the chill,
So drink John' – and well he wrought that night at Bunker's Hill

The battle of Bunker's Hill viewed from above the American position.
Canvas, 27 x 40 ins.

236 *LORD NELSON IN THE 'VANGUARD'
At Naples after the Battle of the Nile, 1798
Canvas, 40 x 60 ins.
Exhib. R.S.M.A., Guildhall, London, 1976

237 THE FRUITER 'PARGA'
Canvas, 16 x 34 ins.

238 THE CONFEDERATE CRUISER 'ALABAMA' SINKING AFTER THE FIGHT WITH THE CRUISER 'KEARSAGE'
The British yacht *Deerhound* rescuing the crew of the *Alabama,* 19th June, 1864
Canvas, 20 x 30 ins.

239 THE U.S. CLIPPER 'ANDREW JACKSON'
Canvas, 20 x 26 ins.

240 U.S. CLIPPER 'EUREKA'
Canvas, 20 x 30 ins.

241 'MISTY DAWN' AT SEA
Canvas, 20 x 27 ins.

242 *THE CALIFORNIAN CLIPPER 'QUEEN OF THE SEAS'
1400 tons (Captain Knight). Built by Paul Curtis, East Boston, in 1852. Owners, Glidden & Williams, Boston.
Now in an American collection

243 THE U.S. CRUISER 'IOWA' OF THE GREAT WHITE FLEET AT RIO DE JANEIRO, 1907
Canvas, 24 x 36 ins.
In the possession of Mr. W. Cramp Scheetz, Junior

The following works were the result of a suggestion put to the artist for a special Bicentennial Exhibition of seascapes depicting American naval engagements during the War of Independence and the years 1775 and 1776. On completion the collection was exhibited in the United States (May 1976) at Wm. Blair Inc., Bethesda, Maryland.

1973 244 JOHN PAUL JONES IN THE 'ALFRED' ESCAPES IN A GALE FROM THE BRITISH FRIGATE 'MILFORD', 8th December, 1776
Early in October Commodore Hopkins had proposed sending a small Squadron to Cape Breton to inflict injury upon the fishery and to attempt the capture of the Coal fleet and release of American prisoners working in the mines. Although the final start was not made until November, the expedition under the command of Paul Jones engaged in several actions which, combined with the depletion of his strength in making up prize crews and the drain on his provisions and water, forced him to form his prizes into a squadron and proceed with them into port. The *Alfred* was the only vessel of the original squadron left and the five prizes left him with barely enough men to guard the prisoners. He finally arrived at Nantasket road with the loss of only one of the prizes, but in a fierce gale during the night of December 8th the British Frigate *Milford* recaptured the ship *John* which Jones had taken on November 26th.
Canvas, 24 x 36 ins.

245 THE AMERICAN SLOOP 'TYRANNICIDE' CAPTURES THE BRITISH SCHOONER 'DESPATCH'
In February 1776 the General Court of Massachusetts authorised the building of ten vessels. The number was later reduced to five. The first completed was *Tyrannicide,* with 14 guns, to be manned by 75 men and rigged as a sloop. Sailing under the command of Captain Fisk on July 8th, 4 days later she fell in with the British armed Schooner *Despatch* from Halifax bound for New York. After 1½ hours the schooner struck. Although *Tyrannicide* was badly knocked about, she took her prize to Salem. 30 men, 8 carriage guns, 12 swivels, 20 small arms, 16 pistols, 20 cutlasses, and other small arms and powder represented no mean haul. Fisk sailed again taking 4 more prizes, one of which was recaptured by a British frigate which chased and nearly caught the *Tyrannicide.* In the light of this experience *Tyrannicide* was changed from a sloop to a brigantine.
Canvas, 24 x 36 ins.

246 GENERAL BENEDICT ARNOLD AT VALCOUR ENGAGES THE BRITISH FLEET, 11th October, 1776

General Arnold, in command of the American Fleet on Lake Champlain, had placed his ships in such a position in the Bay of Valcour that the British had to pass the Island of Valcour before discovering their enemy and were forced to attack from the leeward at a disadvantage. The fight, which began at about 11 a.m., lasted until dark and, although the British were unable to bring any vessels but their gunboats into action, Arnold says he suffered much for want of seamen and gunners and that 'I was obliged myself to point most of the guns aboard the *Congress,* which I believe did good execution.'

Canvas, 24 x 36 ins.

247 PAUL JONES IN THE AMERICAN SLOOP 'PROVIDENCE' OUTMANŒUVRES THE BRITISH FRIGATE 'SOLEBAY', August 1776

John Paul Jones in the sloop *Providence,* sailed from Delaware Bay on August 21st. Down in the latitude of Bermuda he fell in with the British frigate *Solebay,* with 28 guns. She sailed fast and chased the *Providence* for 4 hours, at which point she got within musket shot of the American's quarter. No colours had yet been shown. Jones then hoisted his and began firing, upon which the *Solebay* hoisted American colours too and fired guns to leeward. 'But' says Jones, 'the Bait would not take, for having everything prepared, I bore away before the wind and set all our light sail at once, I was almost out of reach of grape and soon after out of reach of cannon shot.' Jones says that if the *Roebuck* had seen the action taken and had been prepared to counteract it he might have fired several broadsides of double-headed and grape shot, which would have done the *Providence* very material damage. As it was, not one of the many shots fired hit the American ships.

Canvas, 24 x 36 ins.

248 CAPTAIN BIDDLE IN THE AMERICAN BRIG 'ANDREW DORIA' CAPTURES TWO BRITISH TRANSPORTS, 29th May, 1776

At 4 a.m. Captain Nicholas Biddle in the 14-gun brig *Andrew Doria* discovered two ships, and two hours later he brought them to. They were the transports *Crawford* and *Oxford,* which between them had 217 Highland troops on board, as well as some women and children. All these people were put into the *Oxford*; and a prize crew of 11 men, with Lieutenant James Josiah in command, took over the *Crawford.* This was one of many actions that resulted in a loss of troops which caused the British considerable worry.

Canvas, 24 x 36 ins.

1974 249 THE BRITISH FRIGATE 'ACTÆON' DESTROYED IN CHARLESTON HARBOUR, 28th June, 1776

During the British attack on Charleston, three ships – *Sphynx, Actæon,* and *Syren* – were to have been to the westward of the main force facing the fort. It was intended that these three ships should prevent the fire ships and other vessels from annoying the ships engaged, that they should enfilade the works, and that they should cut off the retreat of the rebels if they should be driven from the fort. The three frigates were unable to manage this service, however, as the pilot who was to take them into position only succeeded in running them aground. *Sphynx* and *Syren* got off in a few hours. *Actæon* remained fast, and in the morning the Captain and Officers scuttled her and set her on fire. Afterwards the Americans boarded her and took her colours and other property. Half an hour later she blew up.

Canvas, 24 x 36 ins.

250 A BRITISH SCHOONER CAPTURED AT HOG ISLAND, May 27th 1775

The islands in Boston Harbour had long been used by the colonists for pasturage and were well stocked with cattle and sheep, which the British troops in the town took measures to secure for their own use. Soon after the Battle of Lexington, they carried off all the live-

stock from Governor's and Thompson's islands. The Americans, with the intention of forestalling similar raids, landed between two and three hundred men on Hog Island. These men attempted to bring off the cattle and sheep while a detachment of about thirty crossed over to Noddles Island (East Boston) to do the same, when about one hundred British regulars landed there and chased the Americans back to Hog Island and then began to fire upon them. An armed schooner and a number of barges came up to Hog Island to prevent the people leaving, but were unable to do so. The barges then attempted to tow the schooner back, as there was little wind and a flood tide. The Americans rained a heavy fire of small arms on the barges, and two three-pounders coming to their assistance soon made the barges give up and carry off the schooner's crew. The Americans burned her the next day.
Canvas, 24 x 36 ins.

251 TWO AMERICAN SLOOPS RE-CAPTURED FROM THE BRITISH SLOOP 'FALCON', May, 1775
Early in May, the British sloop-of-war *Falcon,* with 16 guns and under the command of Captain John Linzee seized two American sloops in Vineyard Sound. This was too much for the local folk, who fitted out two vessels and went in pursuit. They retook the two sloops and brought them into a harbour and sent the prisoners to Taunton jail. Such little affairs were quite common, and for some years the people of the Colonies had struggled against the imposition of new customs duties and the enforcement of the Navigation laws.
Canvas, 24 x 36 ins.

252 CAPTAIN LINZEE IN THE BRITISH SLOOP 'FALCON' LOSES TWO PRIZE SCHOONERS, 9th August, 1775
Off Cape Ann, the British sloop-of-war *Falcon,* with 16 guns under the command of Captain John Linzee, fell in with two schooners from the West Indies bound for Salem. One was soon brought to; the other, with a favouring wind, made Gloucester harbour. Linzee, having caught the one, now chased the second, bringing his capture with him. He anchored and sent two barges, with fifteen men in each, and the whale boat, with a Lieutenant and six privates, to take the schooner in the harbour, The local militia and other folk put up a spirited resistance, killing three men and wounding the lieutenant, who then returned. Linzee then bombarded the town, hoping to bring the people to a different frame of mind; but, although the cannon balls went through the houses in all directions, not a soul was hurt in any way. The action lasted several hours. The men at the waterside soon made themselves masters of both schooners, the cutter, the two barges, the boat and every man in them. They lost two men killed and one wounded. They took thirty-five of Linzee's, one of whom blew himself up in an attempt to fire the town.
Canvas, 27 x 40 ins.

253 COMMODORE HOPKINS LANDS AT FORT NASSAU, March, 1776
Commodore Hopkins' fleet, which arrived at Abaco on March 1st, consisted of the *Alfred* (24 guns), the *Columbus* (20 guns), the brigs *Andrew Doria* and *Cabot*, the sloops *Providence* and *Hornet* and the schooners *Fly* and *Wasp.* Hopkins intended to capture a quantity of powder known to be stored on the island, a commodity of which the Americans were in sore need. But on the 3rd he landed 200 marines and 50 sailors on New Providence at a place called New Guinea. They captured Fort Montague and spent the night in it. Having heard that there were over 200 men at the main fort, he sent a message to say that all persons and property would be safe, providing there was no opposition. In the morning they took possession of the fort, and the fleet that had been waiting came into the harbour; the Commodore and Captains landed and went up to the fort. Although the powder had been sent away before they arrived, they did acquire a mass of stores.
Canvas, 30 x 45 ins.

254 *THE 'DEFENCE' CHASES THE BRITISH SLOOP 'OTTER' DOWN CHESAPEAKE BAY AND RECAPTURES HER PRIZES, March, 1776

Delaware Bay, Chesapeake Bay, and the coastal waters of the Carolinas saw many a marine conflict take place on their waters in 1776. Pennsylvania, Maryland and Virginia had many small and large vessels for defence, and a number of captures were made early in the year. In March the British sloop-of-war *Otter,* with several tenders and prizes, came up Chesapeake Bay almost as far as Baltimore. The ship *Defence,* under the command of Captain James Nicholson of the Maryland Navy, went out to meet the *Otter,* drove her down the Bay, and captured her prizes.

Canvas, 30 x 50 ins.

255 THE BRITISH SHIPS 'ROEBUCK' AND 'LIVERPOOL', ATTACKED BY THIRTEEN PENNSYLVANIAN GALLEYS AND THE SCHOONER 'WASP', May, 1776

The British man-o'-war *Roebuck* (44 guns) cruised about the Virginia and Delaware Capes from the middle of March until June. On the 8th May, in the company of the *Liverpool* (28 guns) and a number of tenders and prizes, she came up Delaware Bay and was met below Chester Bay by 13 Pennsylvanian galleys. An engagement followed, which lasted all afternoon. The Continental schooner *Wasp* came out of Christiana Creek, into which she had been driven the day before by the British, and recaptured one of their prizes, a brig. The *Roebuck,* considerably injured in her rigging, was grounded on a shoal while trying to get near the galley. The *Liverpool* anchored nearby for her protection. During the night the *Roebuck* got off and the British dropped down river. The galleys attacked again the next day.

Canvas, 40 x 60 ins.

1975 256 THE BRITISH FLEET EVACUATES BOSTON, 14th June, 1776

After waiting in Boston Harbour for 3 months after the evacuation of the town by the British troops, the men-of-war, with some transports, set sail for Halifax. This fleet, commanded by Commodore Banks, consisted of 8 ships, 2 snows, 2 brigs, and a schooner. General Ward wrote to General Washington on June 16th, 'The 13th instant at evening I ordered 500 men with proper officers, a detachment of the train with a thirteen-inch mortar, 2 eighteen-pounders and some small cannon under the command of Col. Whitcomb, to take post on Long Island to annoy the enemy ships; the necessary works were thrown up in the night and the next morning our cannon and mortar began to play upon the pirates, which soon drove them all out of the harbour. . . .' They blew up the lighthouse as they went off and then put to sea with their fleet.

Canvas, 40 x 60 ins.

257 THE AMERICAN SLOOP 'UNITY' CAPTURES THE SCHOONER 'MARGARETTA', 12th June, 1775

When Captain Ichabod Jones brought provisions from Boston to exchange for lumber at Machias, the patriots in that place, who were mostly for the provincial cause, would have none of the bargain. Under the lead of Benjamin Foster and Jeremiah O'Brien, action was taken against Jones, who fled to the woods but was later captured. The provisions had been brought on two sloops – the *Unity* and the *Polly* – escorted by the armed schooner *Margaretta,* under the command of Lieutenant Moore, who threatened to bombard the town. The local men took possession of the two sloops and followed the *Margaretta*; in a skirmish, the *Polly* had to be run aground. In the morning of the 12th the *Margaretta* took the skipper of a small sloop for a pilot; robbed another of gaff and boom, provisions, and a Mr. Robert Avery; and proceeded to sea. Then about 40 men from the town armed themselves with guns, swords, axes and pitchforks and put to sea in the *Unity.* They built breastworks of

pine boards and anything they could find for screens. In the action that followed, the *Unity* ran her bowsprit through the *Margaretta's* main shrouds and drove the crew below. The British lost 11 men killed and wounded as well as the *Polly,* which had 14 guns.
Canvas, 24 x 36 ins.

258 CAPTAIN JOHN MANLEY IN THE AMERICAN SCHOONER 'LEE' CAPTURES THE BRITISH BRIGANTINE 'NANCY', 29th November, 1775
Captain John Manley in the 70 ton schooner *Lee* was looking for a British ship that was known to be bound for Boston. He had already, within a period of a few weeks, captured 2 or 3 small vessels and did not want to miss this latest chance. After about a fortnight's search he sighted a sail that proved to be the object of his mission, the brigantine *Nancy,* which surrendered without resistance when overhauled, and was taken into Gloucester. The *Nancy* was carrying a large cargo of ordnance and military stores, a most valuable addition for the American Army. But chief among the items was a thirteen-inch brass mortar, called the 'Congress', which later was used against its original owners.
Canvas, 24 x 36 ins.

259 THE BRITISH BOMBARD THE FORT ON SULLIVAN'S ISLAND, SOUTH CAROLINA, 28th June, 1776
On 4th June the British Fleet under Commodore Parker arrived off the bar at the entrance to Charleston harbour, S.C. The vessels were the *Bristol* (50 guns); *Experiment* (50 guns); the frigates *Solebay, Syren, Active,* and *Actæon* with 28 guns each; the *Sphynx* (20 guns); the *Friendship* (18 guns); the bomb vessel *Thunder* with two mortars; and some small vessels. On 28th the attack was made. A force of 5 or 6 thousand men, all raw troops, and less than half that number regulars, were under the command of General Moultrie. A fort of palmetto logs had been built and was garrisoned by about 350 men and, although bombarded by the British fleet for about ten hours, sustained little damage. The British ships, especially the *Bristol* and *Experiment,* suffered heavy damage and losses, and the fight was not renewed.
Canvas, 24 x 36 ins.

260 *CAPTAIN JAMES TRACEY IN THE AMERICAN BRIG 'YANKEE HERO' CHASES AND ENGAGES THE BRITISH FRIGATE 'MILFORD', 7th June, 1776
Off Cape Ann, Captain James Tracey in the brig *Yankee Hero* with 12 guns and 26 men including officers, sighted a sail and determined to chase. Fourteen men came out in boats to supplement his crew, but even with 40 he had but a third of his complement. He then bore away for the distant ship five leagues away which, too late, he found to be the British frigate *Milford.* Tracey put about for the shore, but the wind dying in the west put *Yankee Hero* at the mercy of the *Milford* which, picking up a fresh southerly, drew up with the American. Within half a mile, the *Milford* fired her bow chasers, and very shortly the most unequal contest was joined. The action lasted over two hours and, although approaching the coast at last, Tracey had to strike with no guns firing and his rigging shot to pieces. Outgunned and outmanned he was forced to see his ship either taken or sunk.
Canvas, 24 x 36 ins.

261 THE BATTLE OF SHIRLEY GUT, 17th May, 1776
Captain Mugford, in the American schooner *Franklin,* captured the ship *Hope* laden with military stores and took her into Boston harbour, in full view of the British fleet at anchor there. This was too much to bear and when Mugford in the *Franklin* and Cunningham in the galley *Lady Washington* sailed out two days later, the British fitted out a flotilla of boats with the intention of surprising and taking them in the night. As the two American vessels were going through Shirley Gut, the *Franklin* went aground and the *Lady Washing-*

ton anchored nearby. The British boats were soon on the scene and, although they had about two hundred men to carry out their plan, the twenty-eight Americans on their two vessels fought so hard with firearms and spears that their enemies soon gave up the contest. Two British boats were sunk and all their men were either killed or drowned. Of the Americans only Captain Mugford was killed, and no men were wounded. The British lost 60 or 70 men and their wounded were not counted. The fight is known as the Battle of Shirley Gut.
Canvas, 24 x 36 ins.

262 GENERAL ARNOLD DESTROYS THE REMAINDER OF HIS LAKE CHAMPLAIN FLEET TO AVOID CAPTURE, 13th October, 1776
After Arnold's courageous fight at Valcour Island on Lake Champlain he knew that his fleet of galleys and gundalows were in no condition to sustain another such contest. At 7 p.m. on the 11th all of his 13 vessels escaped through the British Fleet undetected. Early in the morning of the 12th they anchored at Schylers Island, 10 miles from Valcour. They remained long enough to repair sails and stop leaks and then moved south until, with a freshening breeze, they found the British ships had gained upon them. By the morning of the 13th, Arnold's fleet was separated and the last action began. Two hours later Arnold was forced to run his own galley – the *Congress* – and the last four gundalows on shore. After saving the small arms, the vessels were set on fire.
Canvas, 24 x 36 ins.

1976 263 THE BOSTON TEA PARTY, 16th December, 1773
When in 1773 the East India Company asked the British Government to help them get rid of the great quatities of tea in the warehouses, the Act was passed that empowered the Company to sell this to America without paying the usual English duty. It was thought that the three per cent tax in America would not be noticed. But the Americans realised what was happening and would not accept the proposal. The tea consignees were approached and asked to resign their appointments, but the request was refused. Later, when the imminent arrival of the tea ships was announced, the consignees were again asked to go, and they again refused. When the ships arrived, the law prevented the ships from clearing port until the cargo was discharged. The townsfolk would not allow the unloading, and after twenty days the ships would be liable to seizure. Everyone wanted the tea returned peacefully, but nobody wanted the tea with the tax. The final act is of course universally known; fifty men in full Indian costume emptied 342 boxes of tea from the three vessels into Boston harbour with a huge crowd watching in the moonlight.
Canvas, 27 x 40 ins.

264 CAPTAIN JOHN PAUL JONES IN THE 'BON HOMME RICHARD' ENGAGING AND CAPTURING THE BRITISH FRIGATE 'SERAPIS', 23rd September, 1779
In January 1779 John Paul Jones acquired, at the expense of the French Government, the East Indiaman *Duc de Duras* of 900 tons. The ship was 14 years old and a dull sailer, but the work of converting her to a man-of-war was put in hand at once, and Jones renamed her the *Bon Homme Richard*. A squadron had been formed for a cruise around the British Isles and, after various delays, the squadron set out on 18th August. During the next few weeks small affairs took place; but the final battle was off Scarborough, in which the main contestants were the *Bon Homme Richard* and the British frigate *Serapis*. This was one of the great heroic epics of naval warfare, resulting in the capture of the *Serapis*. Jones's name was assured a place in American history as its greatest naval hero.
Canvas, 24 x 36 ins.

265 FIVE SMALL AMERICAN VESSELS ATTACKING IN THE HUDSON THE BRITISH SHIPS 'PHOENIX' (44 guns) AND 'ROSE' (24 guns), 3rd August, 1776
On August 3rd Lieutenant Colonel Benjamin Tupper reported to General Washington the

result of an operation of a flotilla of five galleys on the Hudson. These were the schooner *General Putnam,* the sloop *Montgomery,* and the galleys *Washington, Lady Washington,* and *Spitfire.* Tupper came up with the British ships *Phœnix* and *Rose* and attacked them at 1.15 p.m. The galleys formed a line and for an hour and a half the *Washington* and *Spitfire* were exposed to the broadsides of the ships. The *Washington* had her bow guns and many of her oars knocked away. The *Lady Washington* had her thirty-two pounder bow gun split for seven inches. The lower tier of one side of the *Phœnix* was equal to that of all the galleys. Yet Tupper resolved on the attack and, as he said, 'for five small gallies to lie near two hours within grape shot of one ship of 44 guns and another of 24 guns is no contemptible affair'.
Canvas, 20 x 40 ins.

266 AMERICANS ATTACKING A BRITISH SLOOP AT MACHIAS
Canvas, 24 x 36 ins.

267 CAPTURE OF A BRITISH SLOOP AT NASSAU
Canvas, 24 x 36 ins.

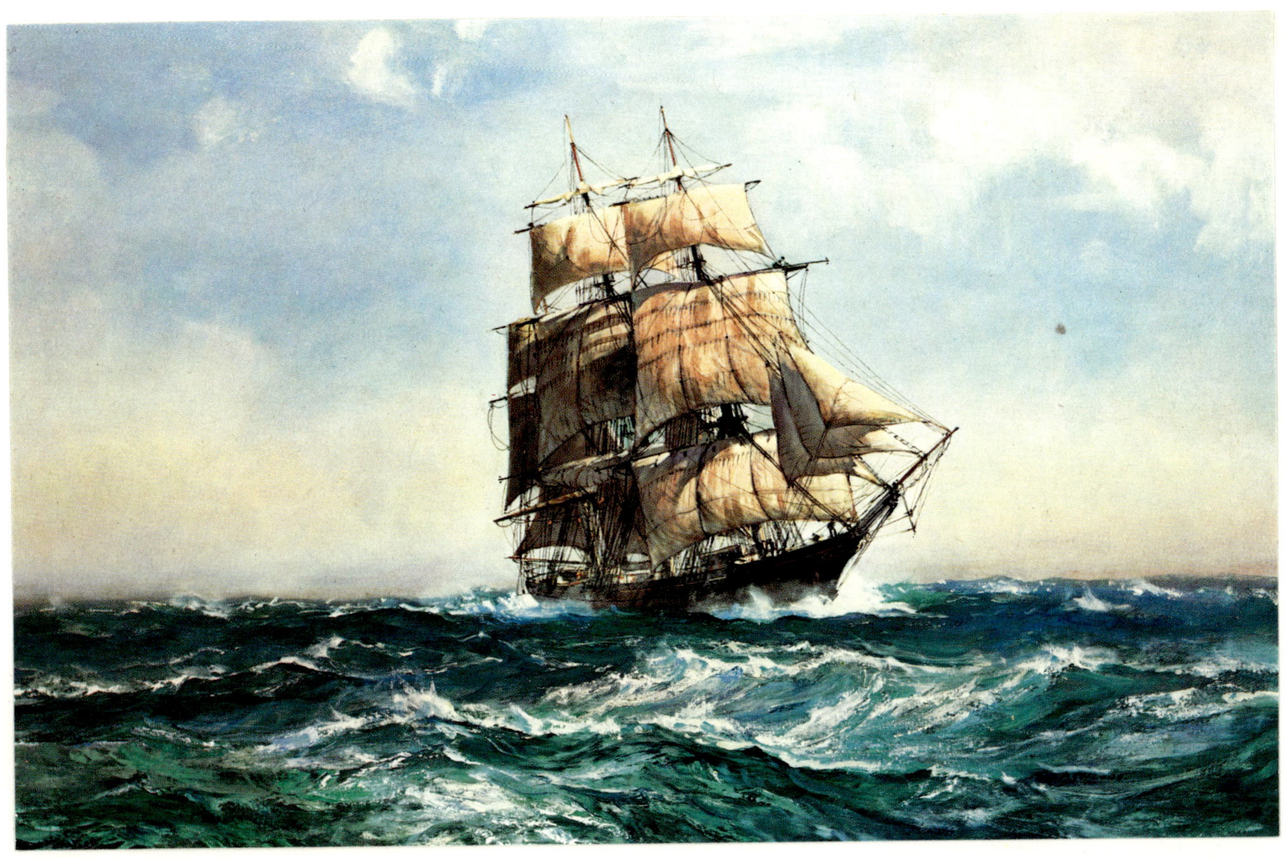

Cat. no. 242* 'QUEEN OF THE SEAS' Canvas, 24 x 36 ins.
In an American collection

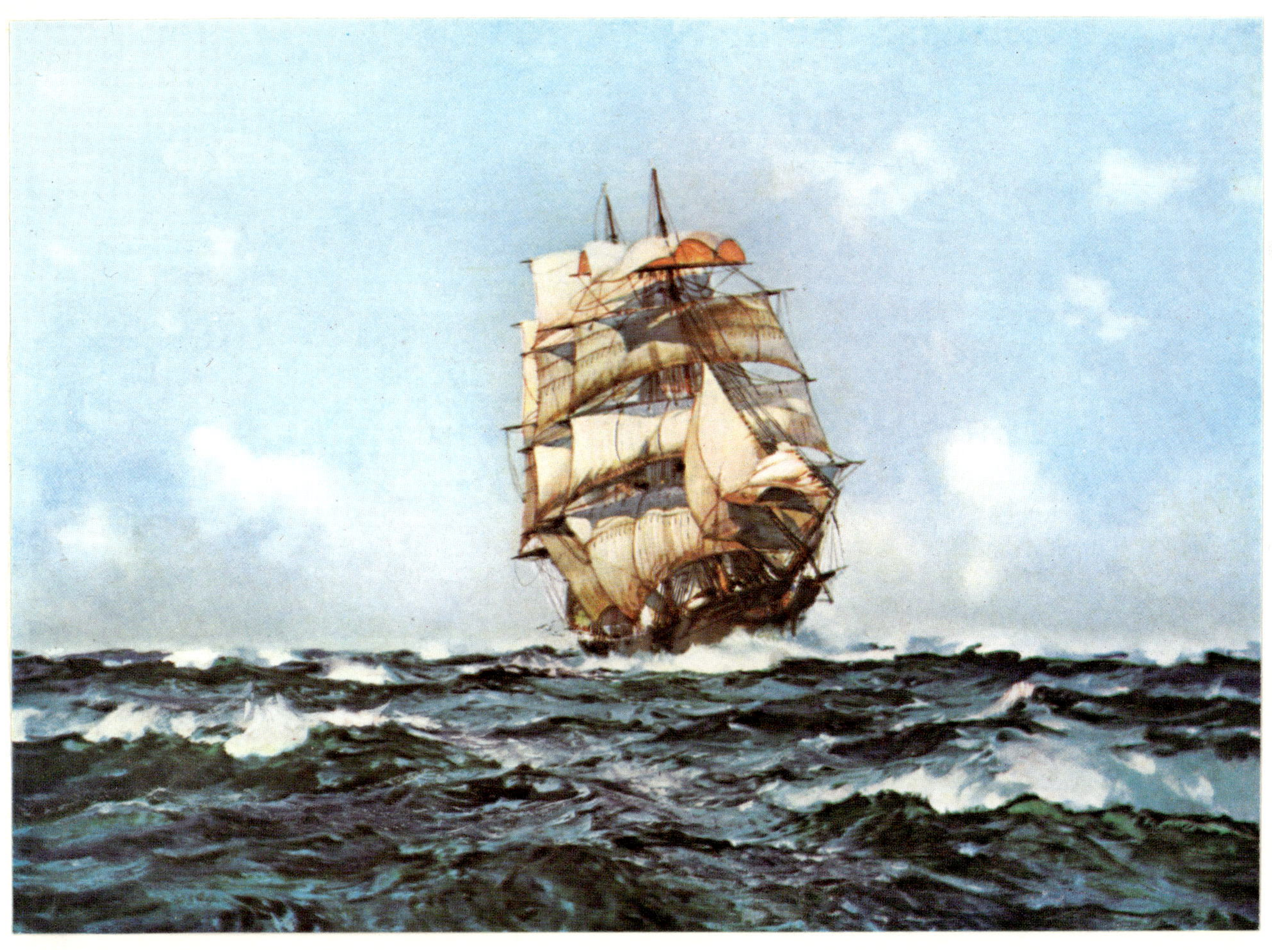

Cat. no. 233* THE AMERICAN CLIPPER 'BLUE JACKET' Canvas

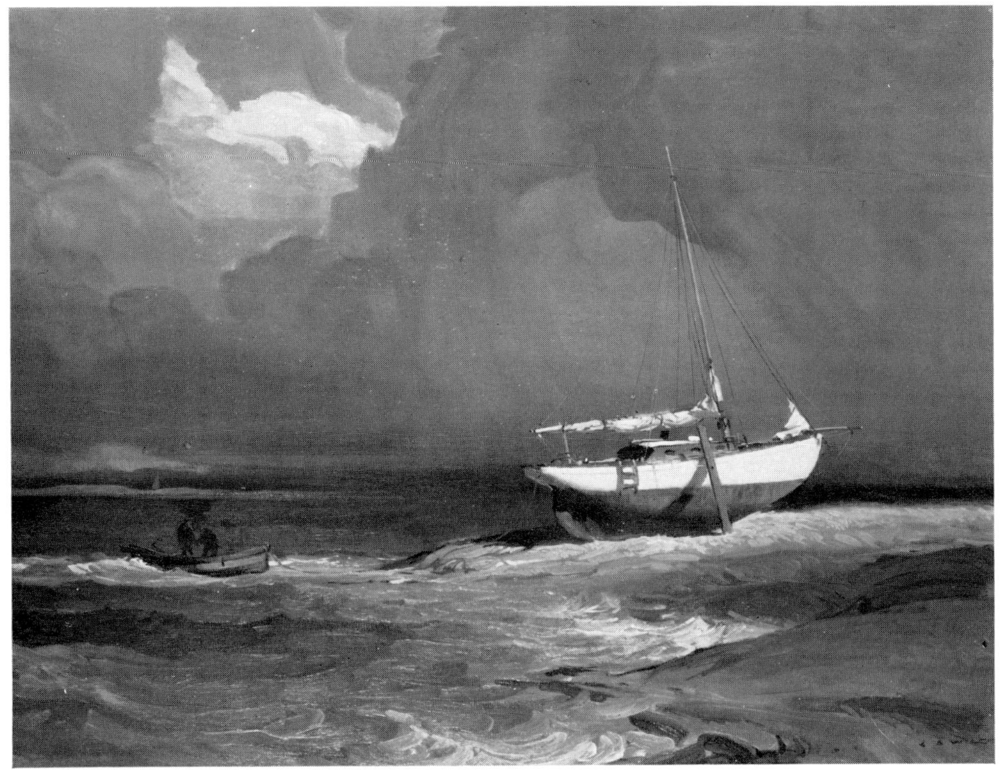

Cat. no. 8 SHIP ASHORE Canvas

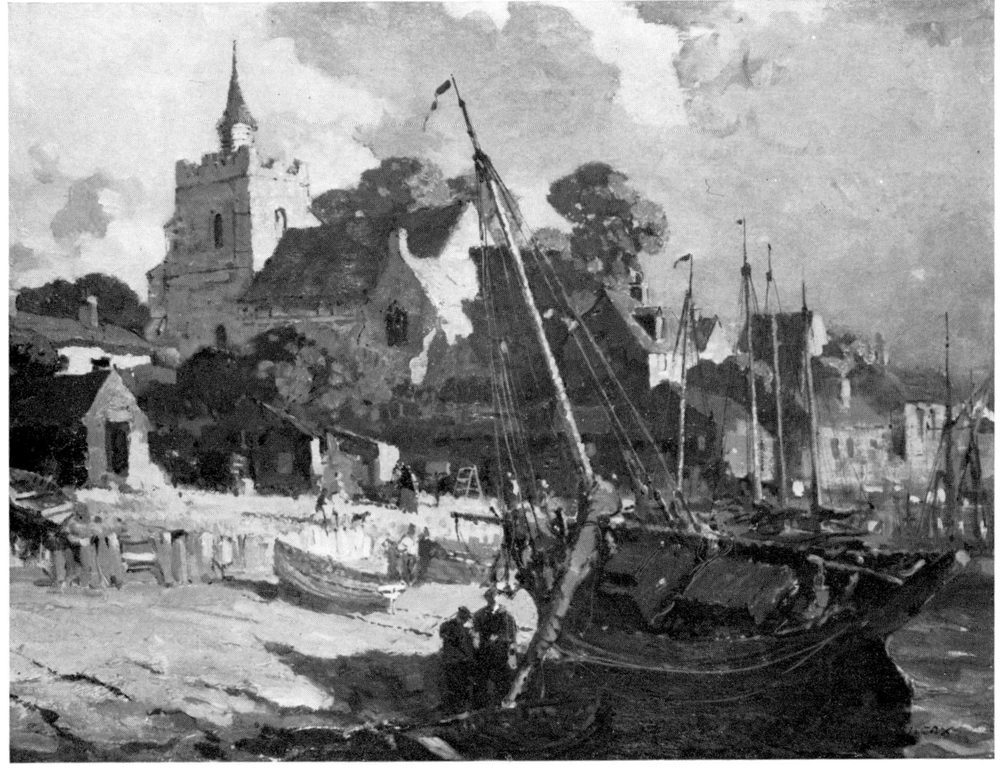

Cat. no. 12 MALDON, ESSEX Canvas, 40 x 50 ins.

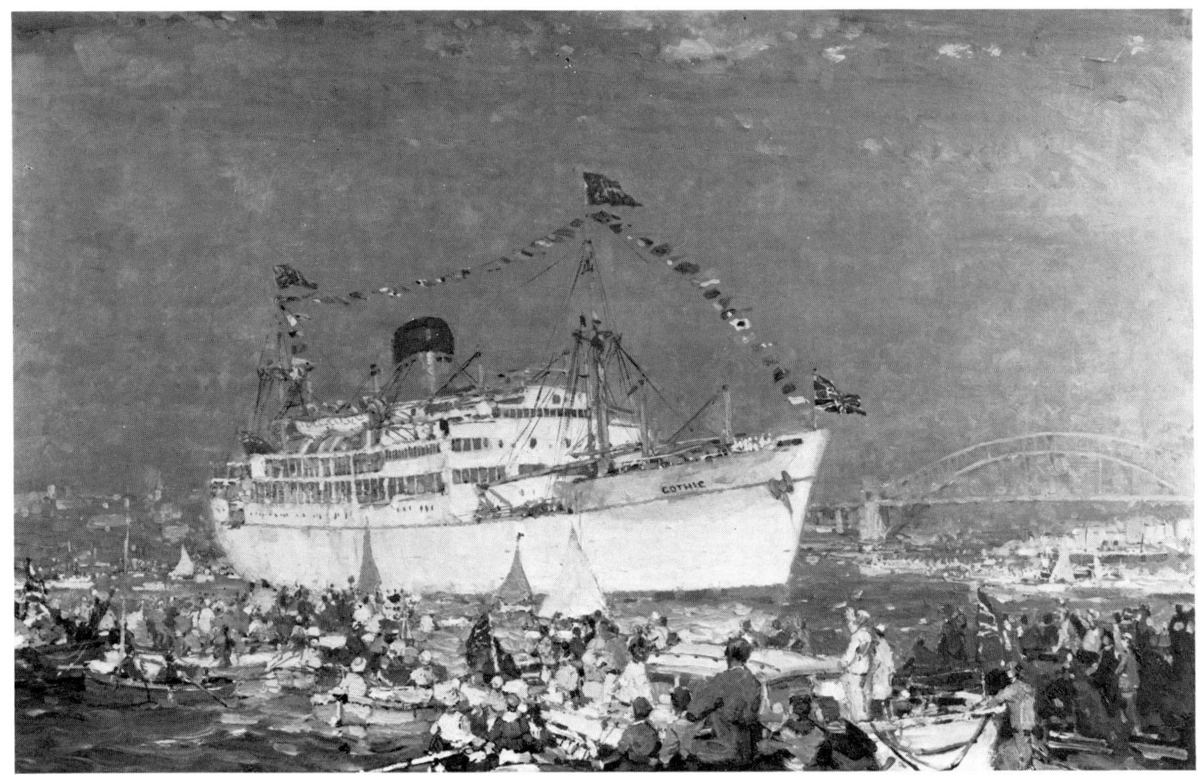

Cat. no. 27 THE 'GOTHIC' AT SYDNEY HARBOUR Canvas, 30 x 40 ins.
In the National Maritime Museum, Greenwich

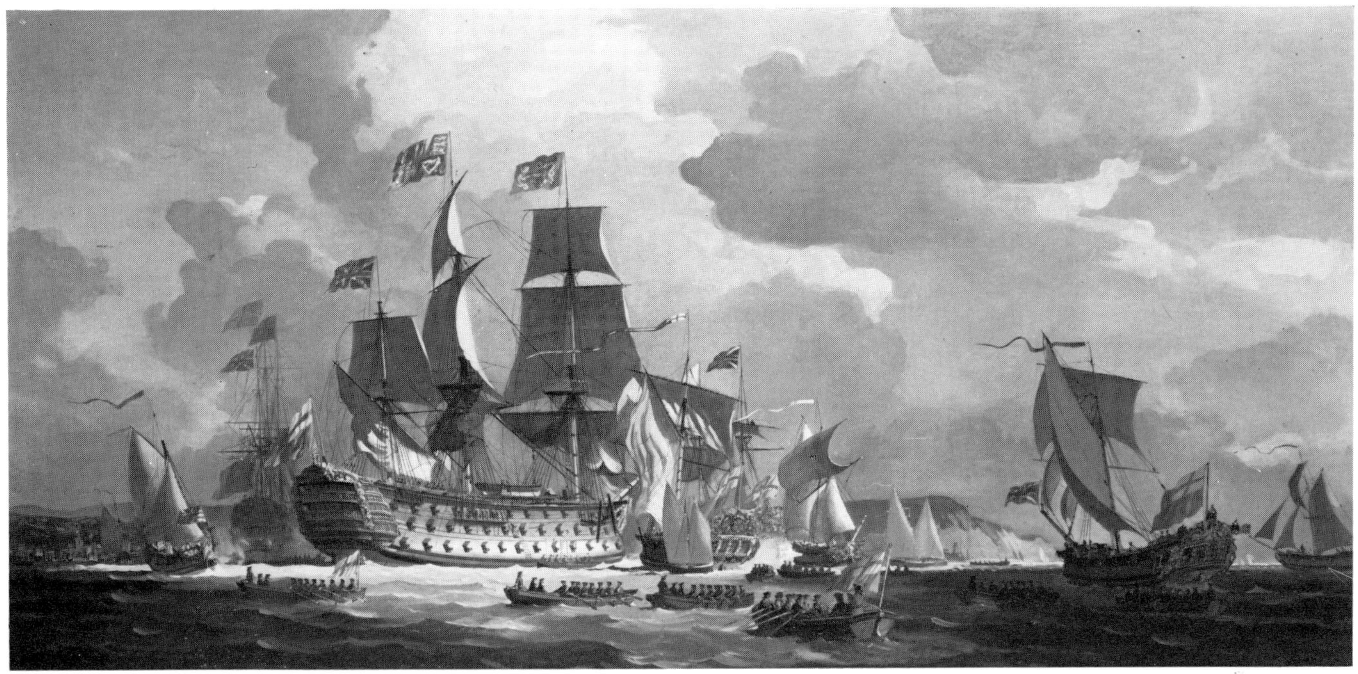

Cat. no. 38 A ROYAL OCCASION Canvas, 30 x 50 ins.

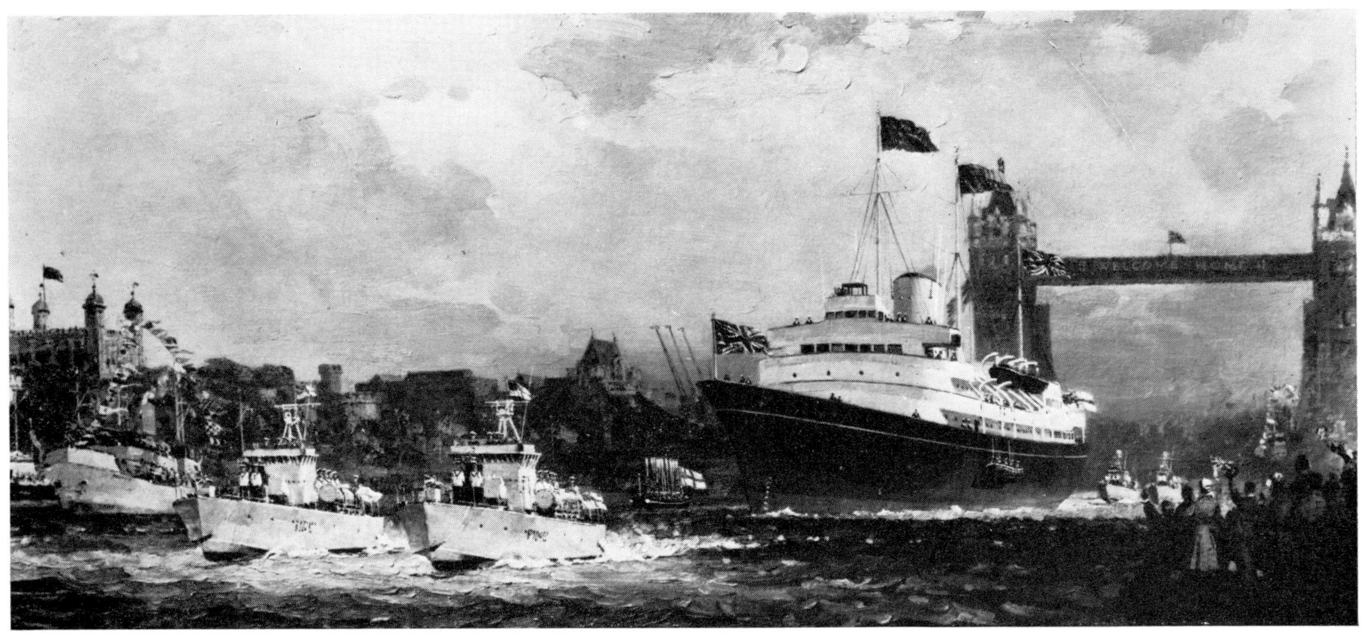

Cat. no. 40 THE RETURN FROM THE COMMONWEALTH TOUR, 1953 Canvas, 26 x 52 ins.
By gracious permission of H.M. The Queen

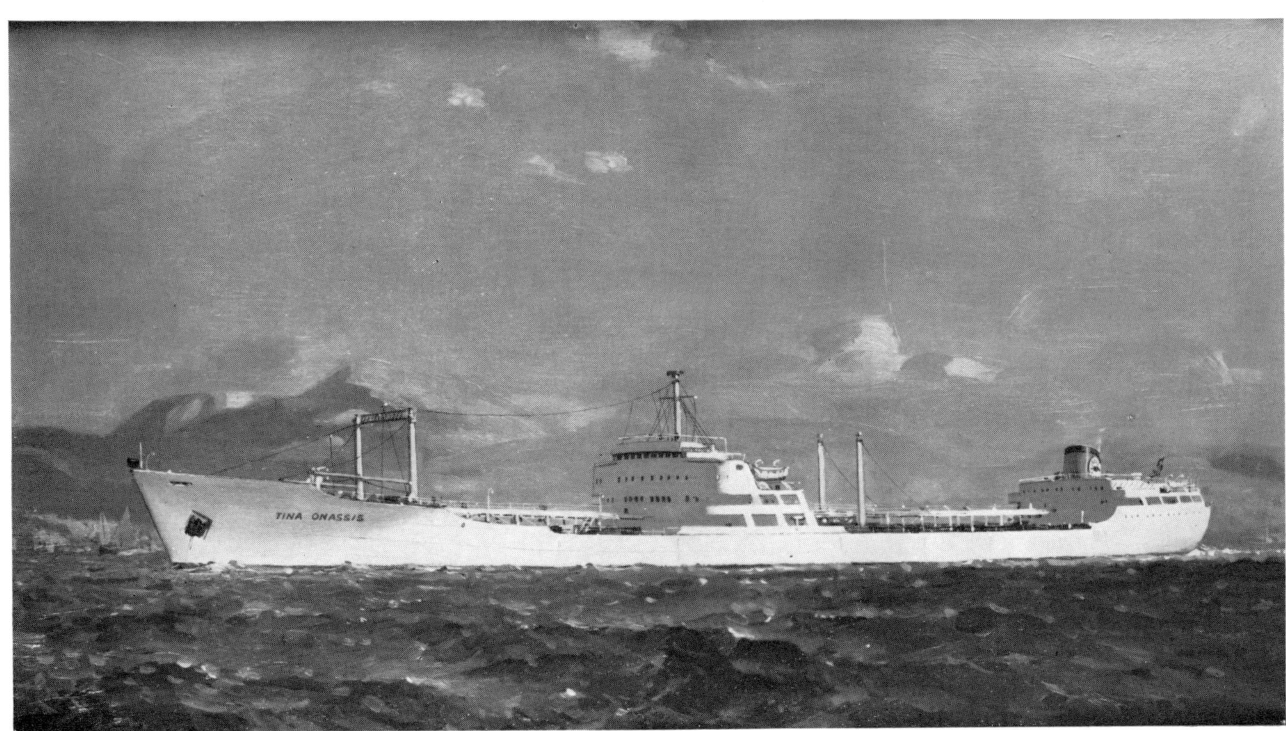

Cat. no. 42 THE TANKER 'TINA ONASSIS' Canvas, 21 x 40 ins.
In the possession of Olympic Maritime

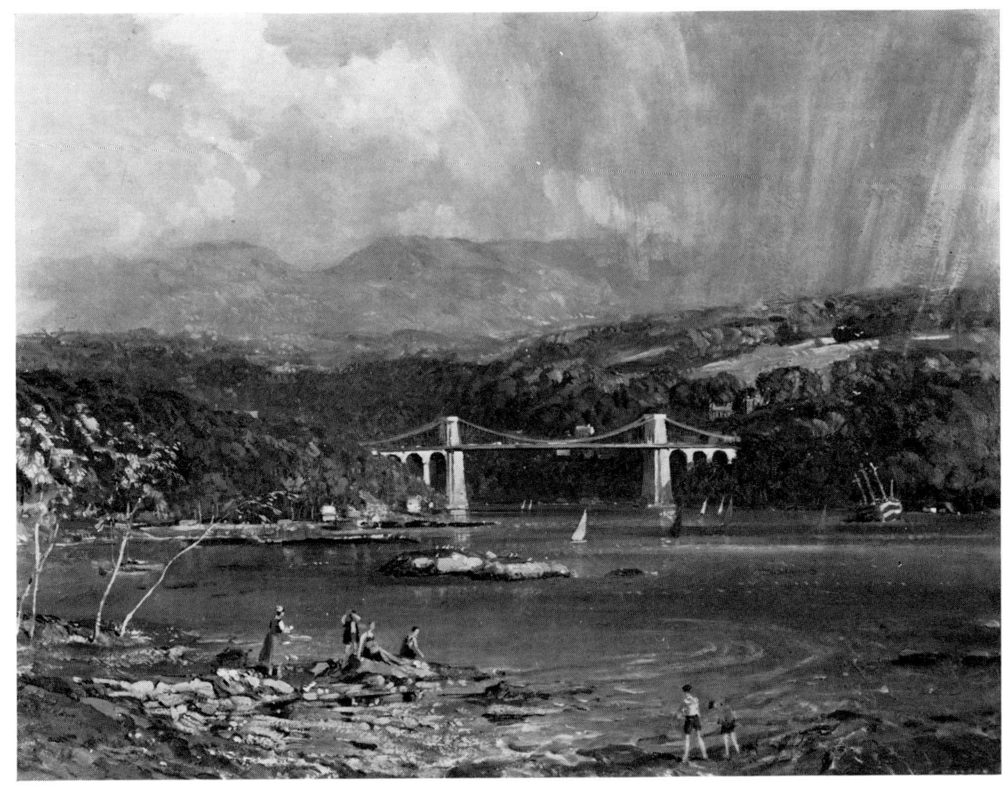

Cat. no. 50 MENAI BRIDGE Canvas, 28 x 36 ins.

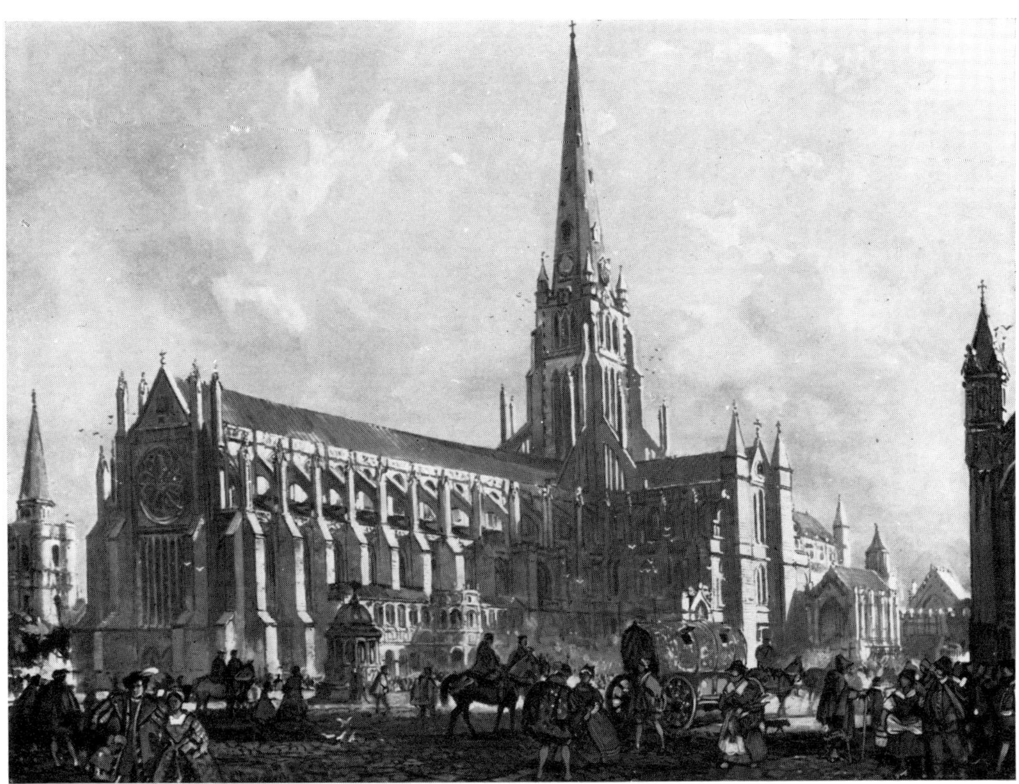

Cat. no. 51 OLD ST. PAUL'S Canvas, 28 x 36 ins.

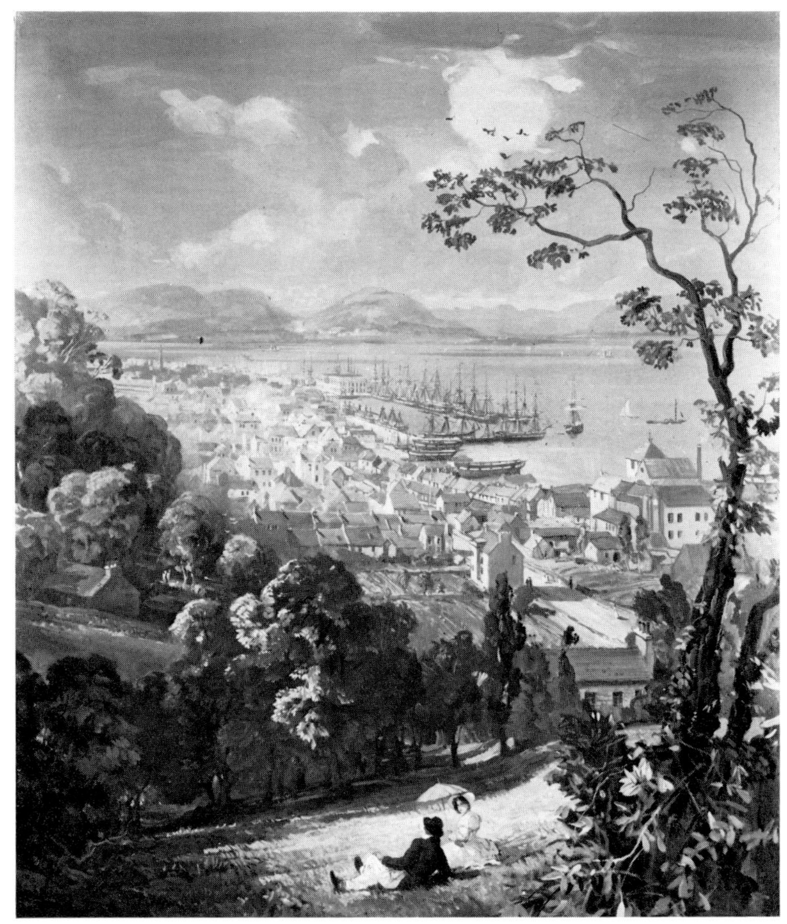

Cat. no. 63 GREENOCK, 1830 Canvas, 72 x 60 ins.
In the possession of British & Commonwealth Shipping Co. Ltd.

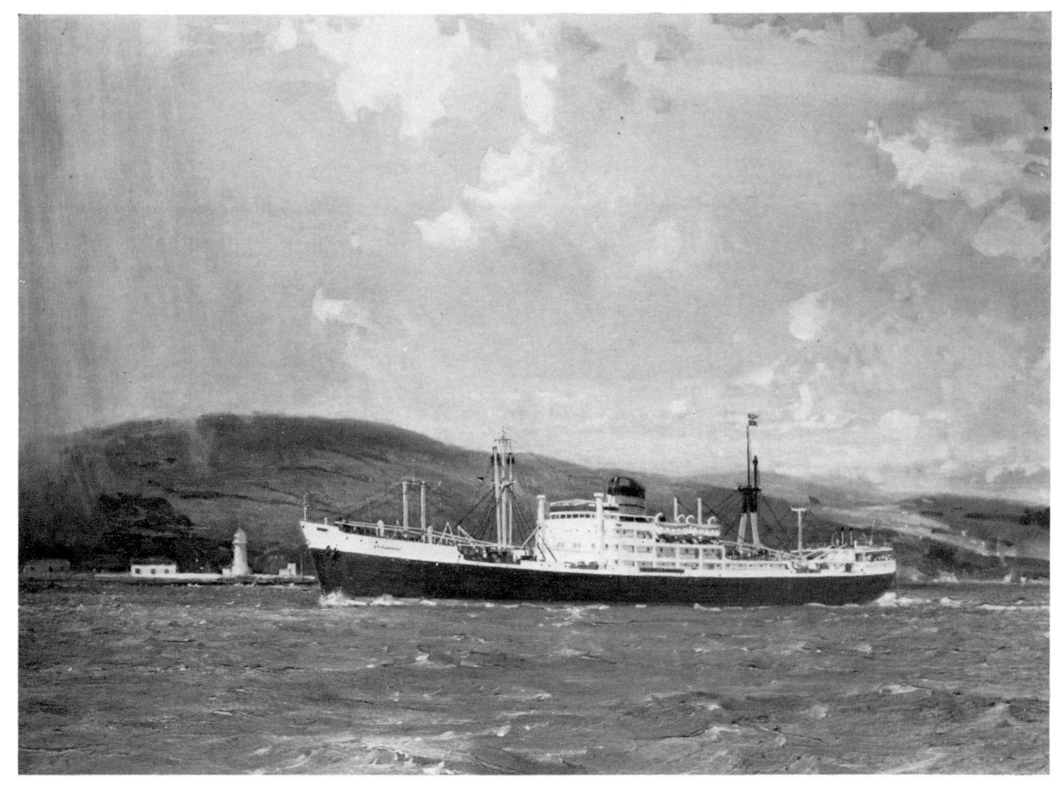

Cat. no. 70 THE 'ARGYLLSHIRE' Canvas, 24 x 36 ins.

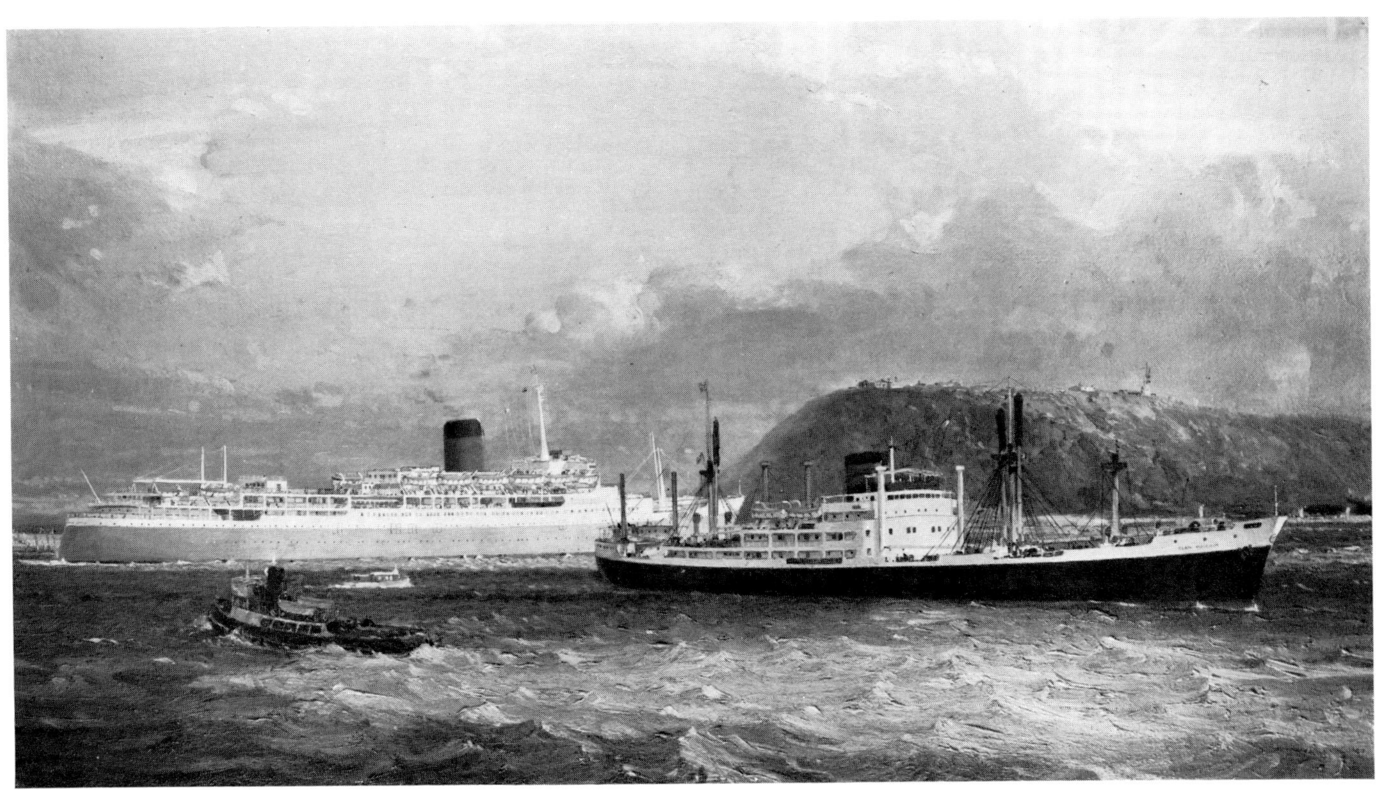

Cat. no. 76 THE 'PENDENNIS CASTLE' & THE 'CLAN MALCOLM' OFF DURBAN Canvas, 30 x 56 ins.
In the possession of Union Castle Mail Steamship Co. Ltd.

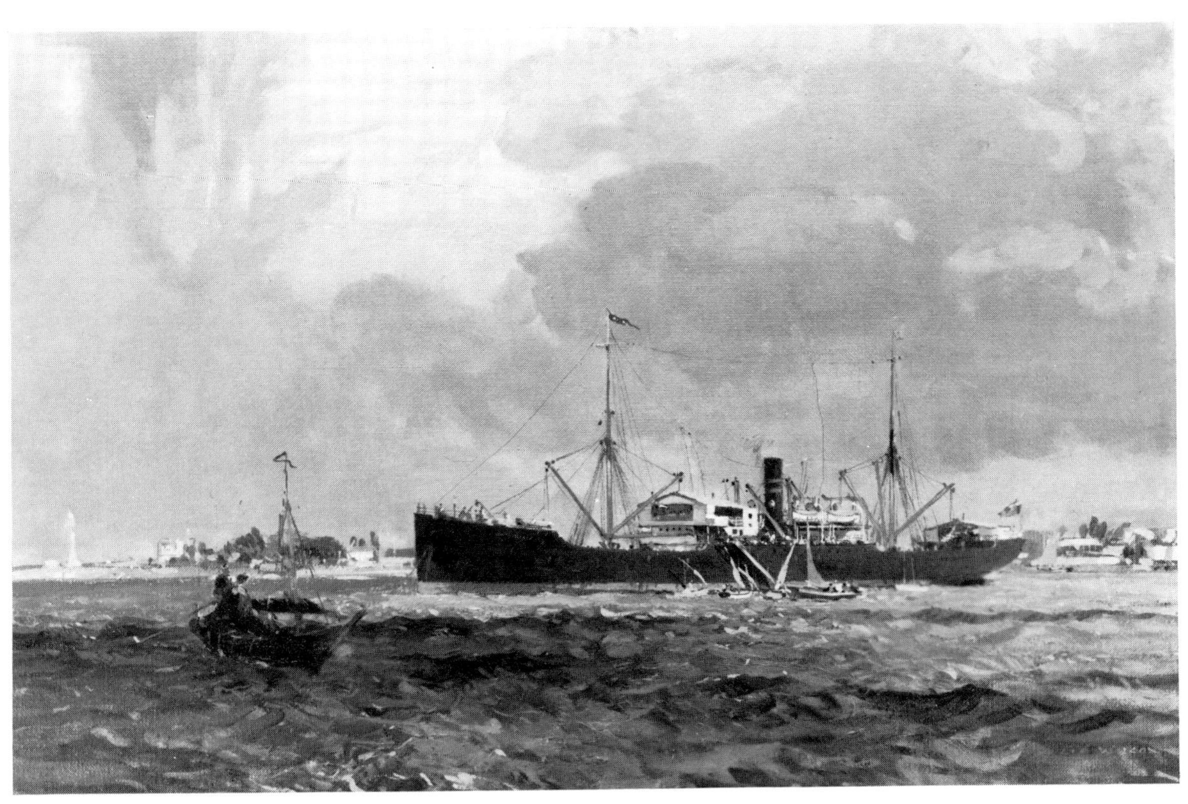

Cat. no. 77 THE 'CLAN SUTHERLAND' AT GALLE Canvas, 24 x 36 ins.
In the possession of the Clan Line Steamers Ltd.

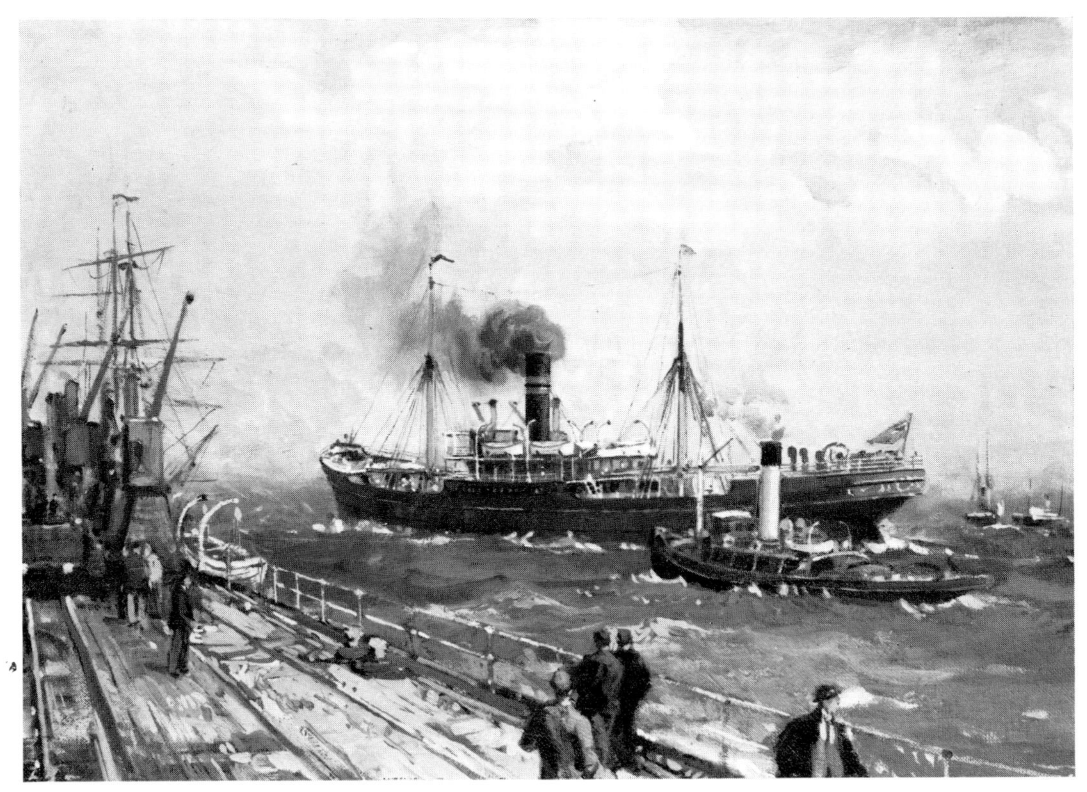

Cat. no. 78 THE 'CLAN OGILVIE' Canvas, 24 x 36 ins.
In the possession of the Clan Line Steamers Ltd.

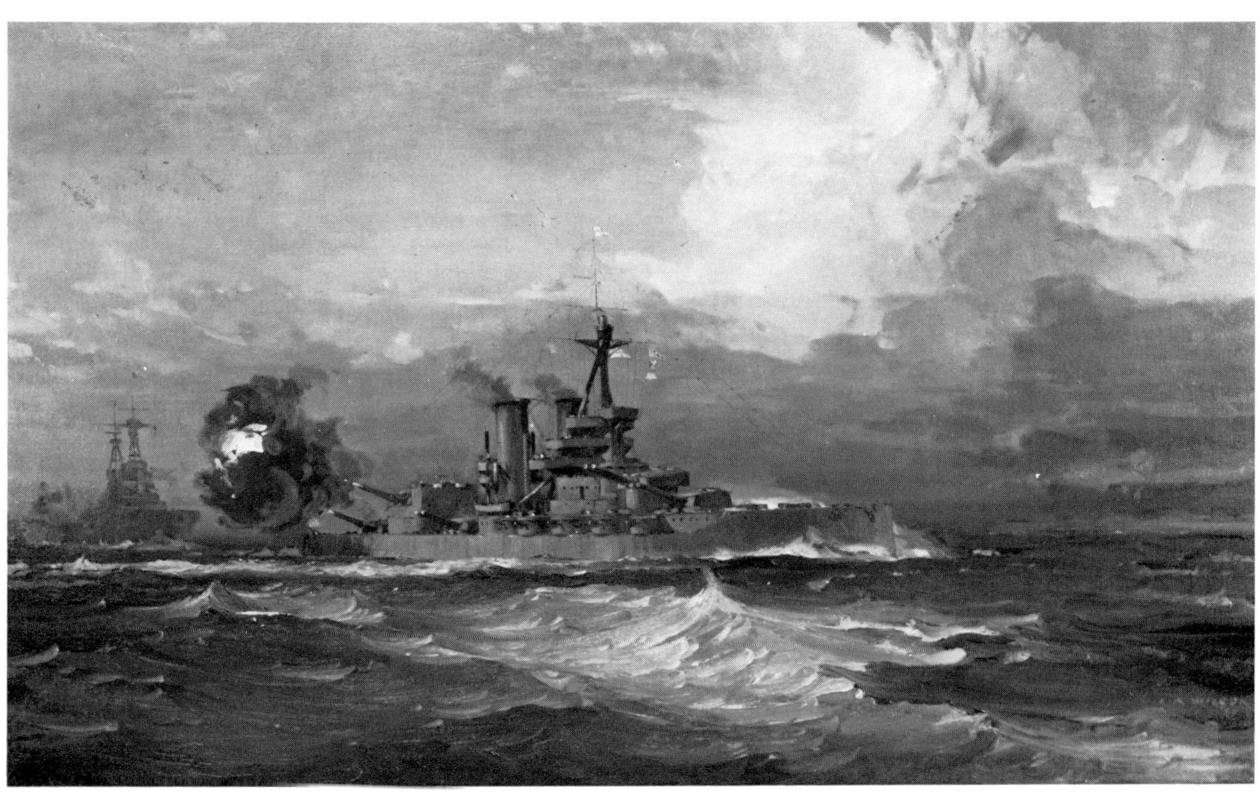

Cat. no. 84 THE BATTLE OF JUTLAND Canvas, 40 x 60 ins.
In the possession of Cayzer Irvine & Co. Ltd.

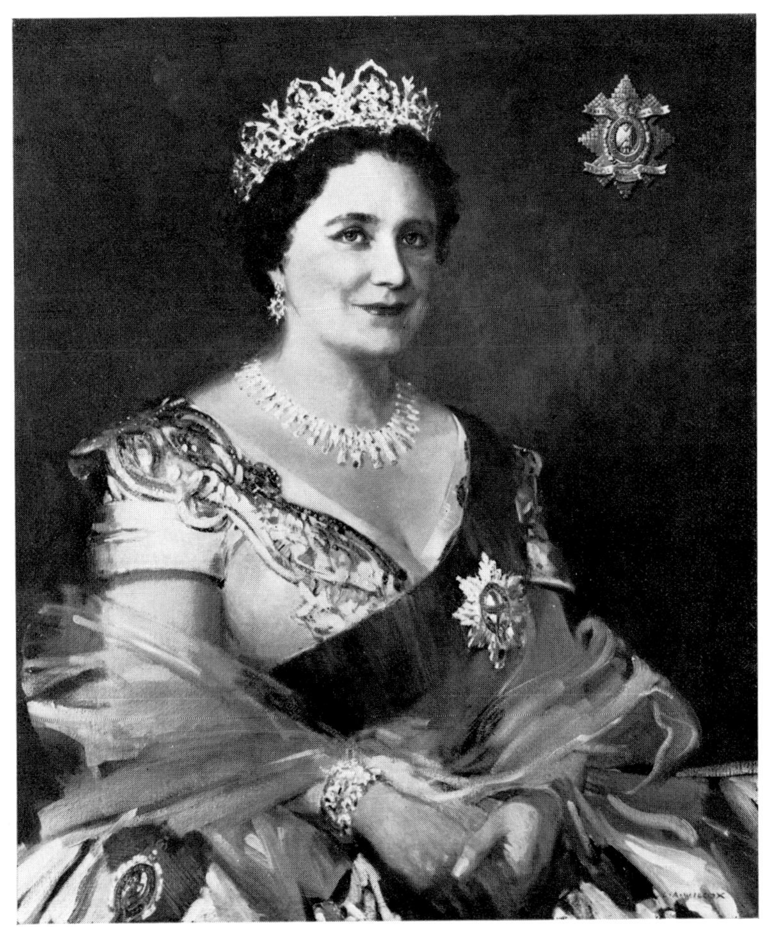

Cat. no. 85 Canvas, 30 x 25 ins.
H.M. QUEEN ELIZABETH, THE QUEEN MOTHER
In the possession of the Black Watch (Royal Highland Regiment) of Canada

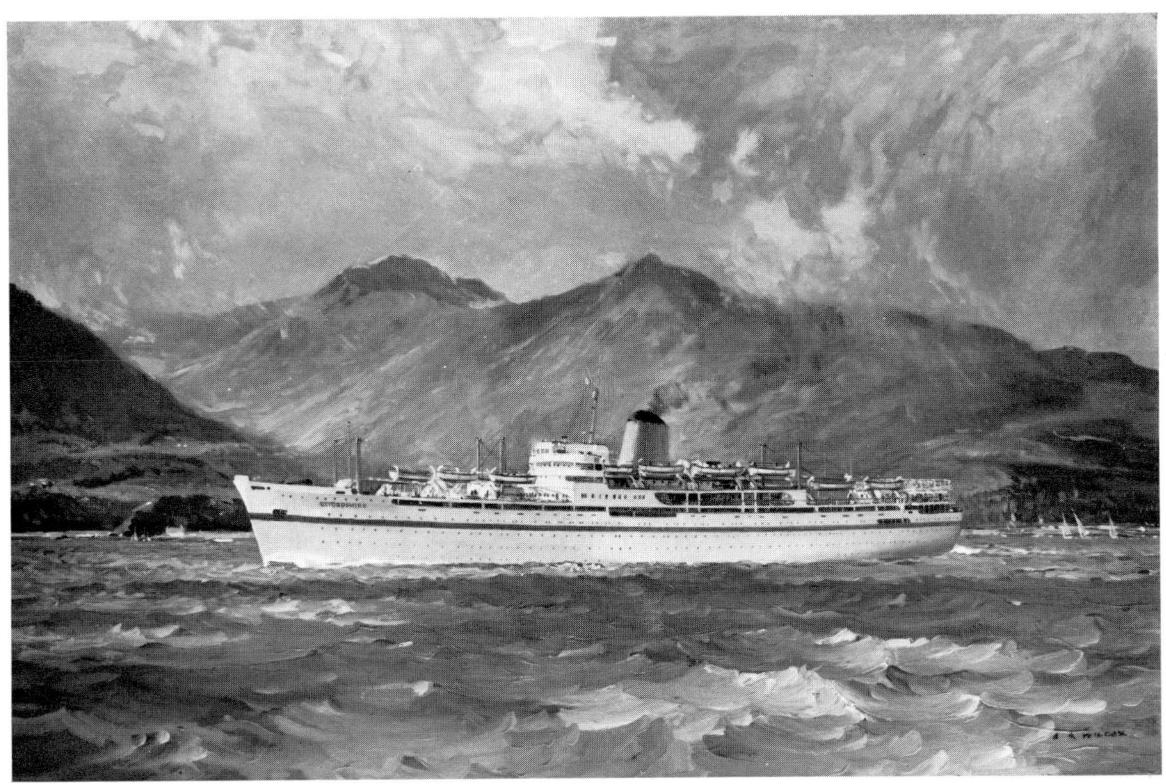

Cat. no. 87 THE TROOPSHIP 'OXFORDSHIRE' Canvas, 36 x 54 ins.
In the possession of the Parker Gallery, London

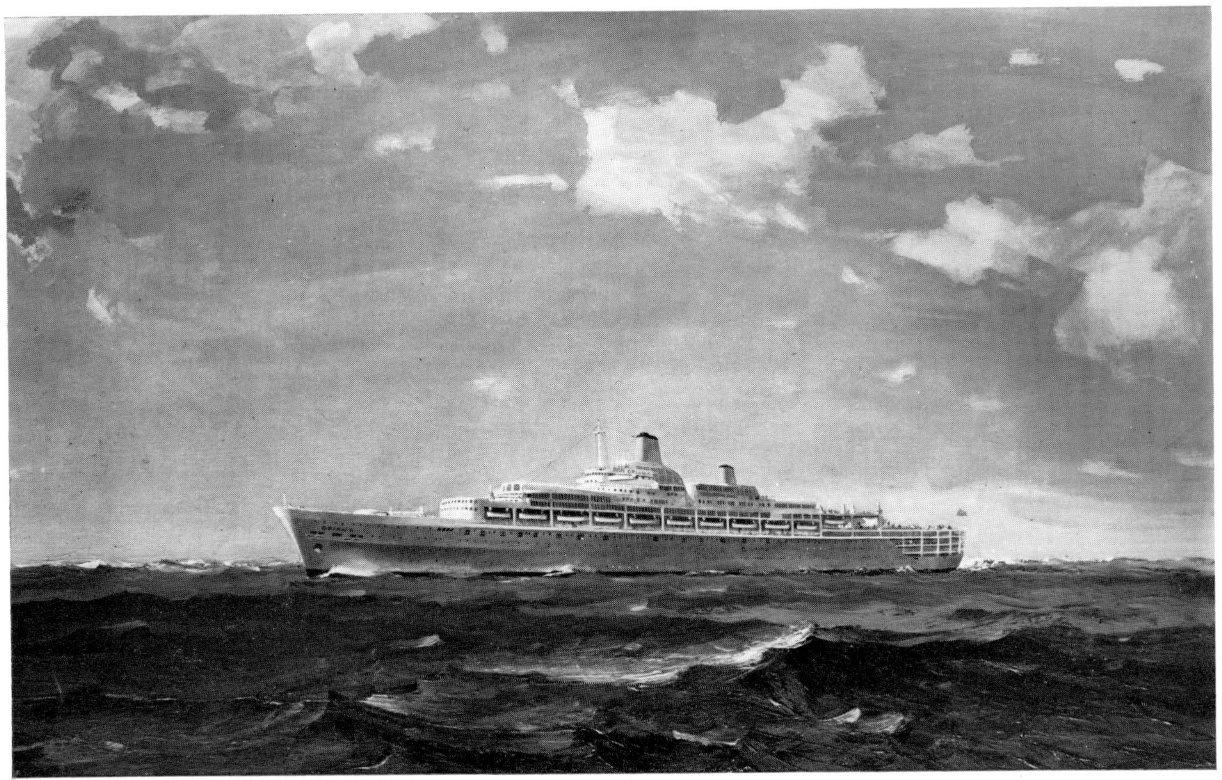

Cat. no. 88 THE 'ORIANA' Canvas, 24 x 36 ins.

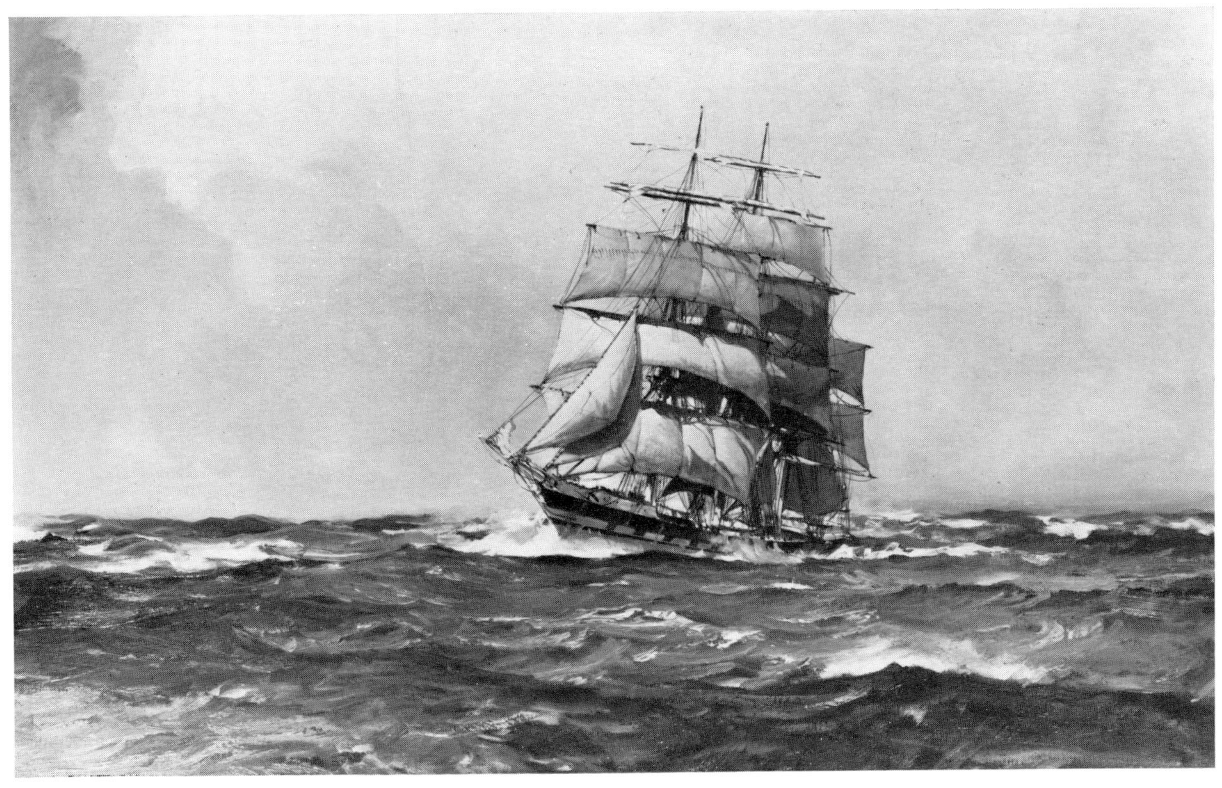

Cat. no. 99 THE CLIPPER SHIP 'MIDDLESEX' Canvas, 24 x 36 ins.

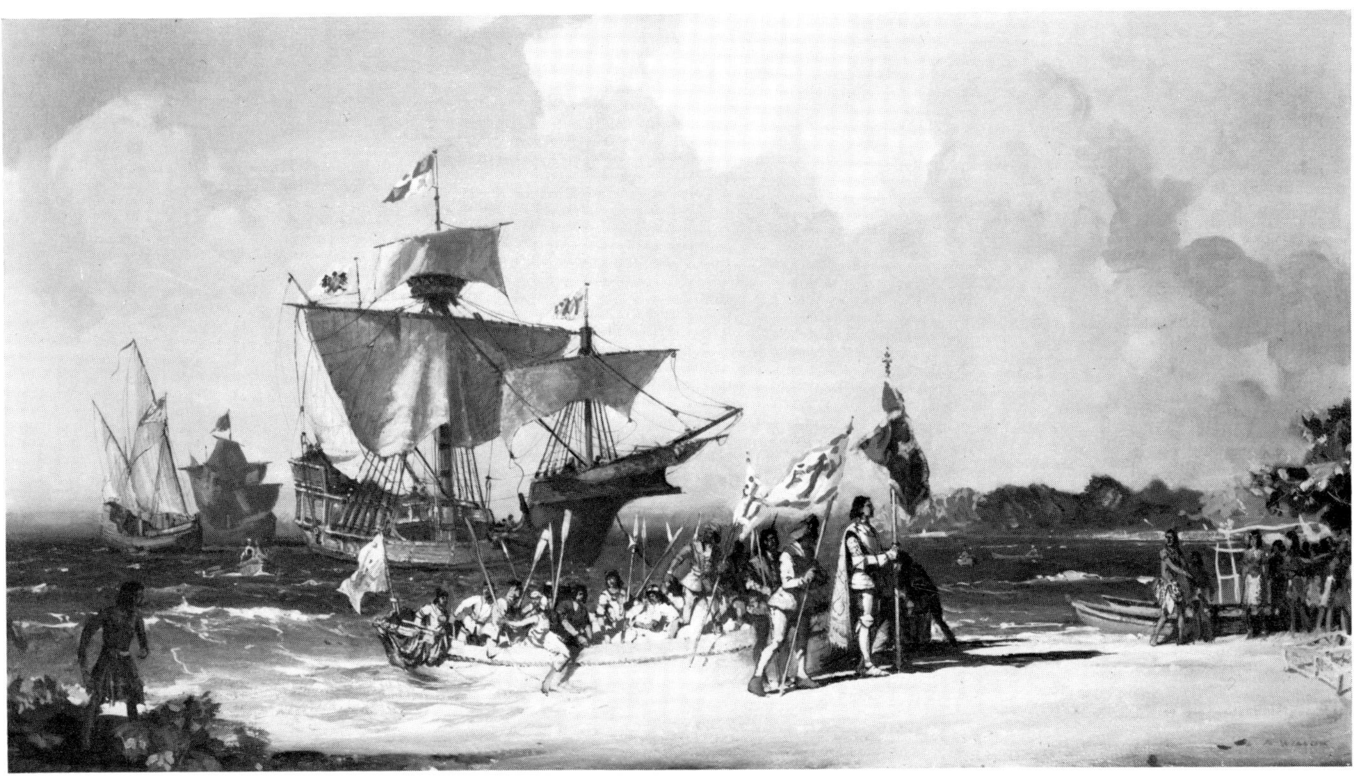

Cat. no. 101 COLUMBUS LANDING (12th October 1492) Canvas, 26 x 40 ins.
Formerly in the possession of the late W. Helweg Larsen

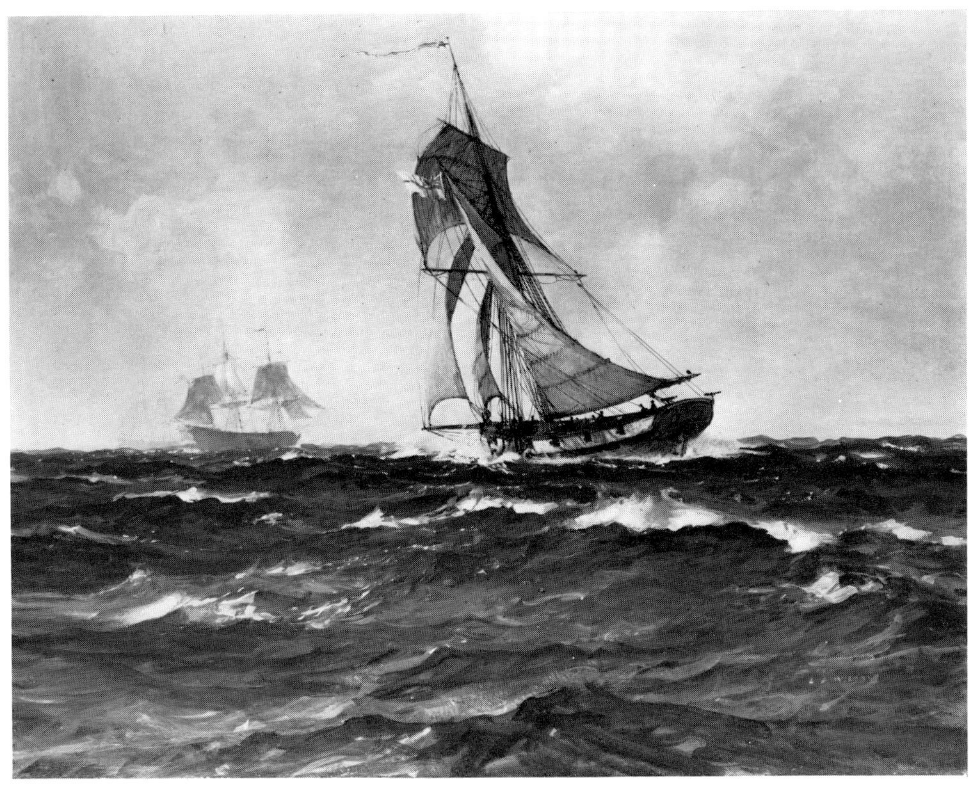

Cat. no. 100 H.M. CUTTER 'ACTIVE' Canvas, 28 x 36 ins.

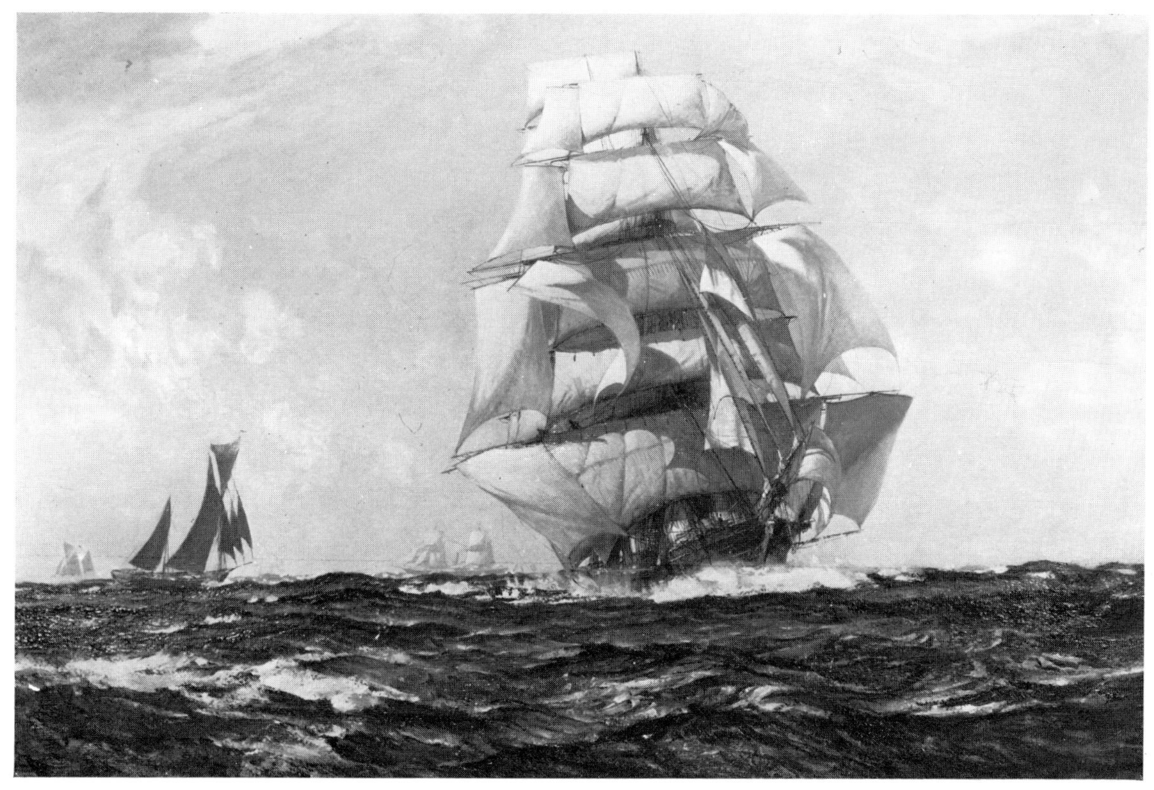

Cat. no. 109 THE GREAT CHINA TEA RACE Canvas, 40 x 60 ins.
In the possession of John Wallrock, Esq.

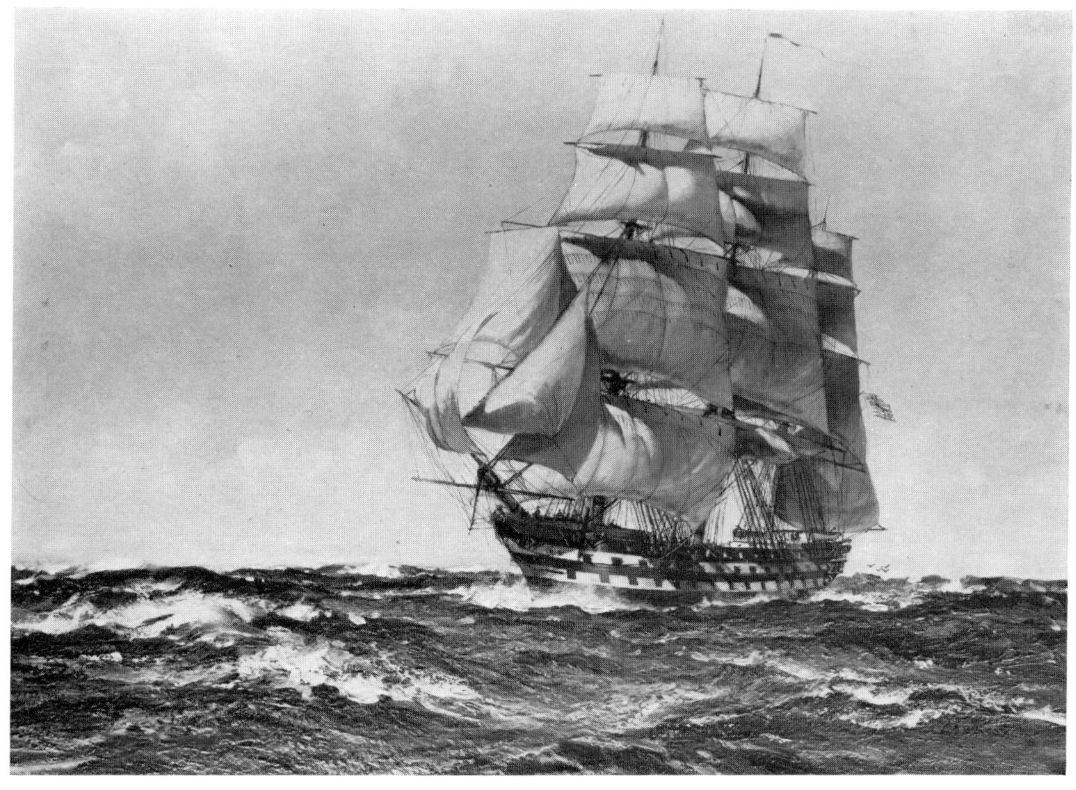

Cat. no. 112 THE EAST INDIAMAN 'EARL OF BALCARRES' Canvas, 30 x 40 ins.

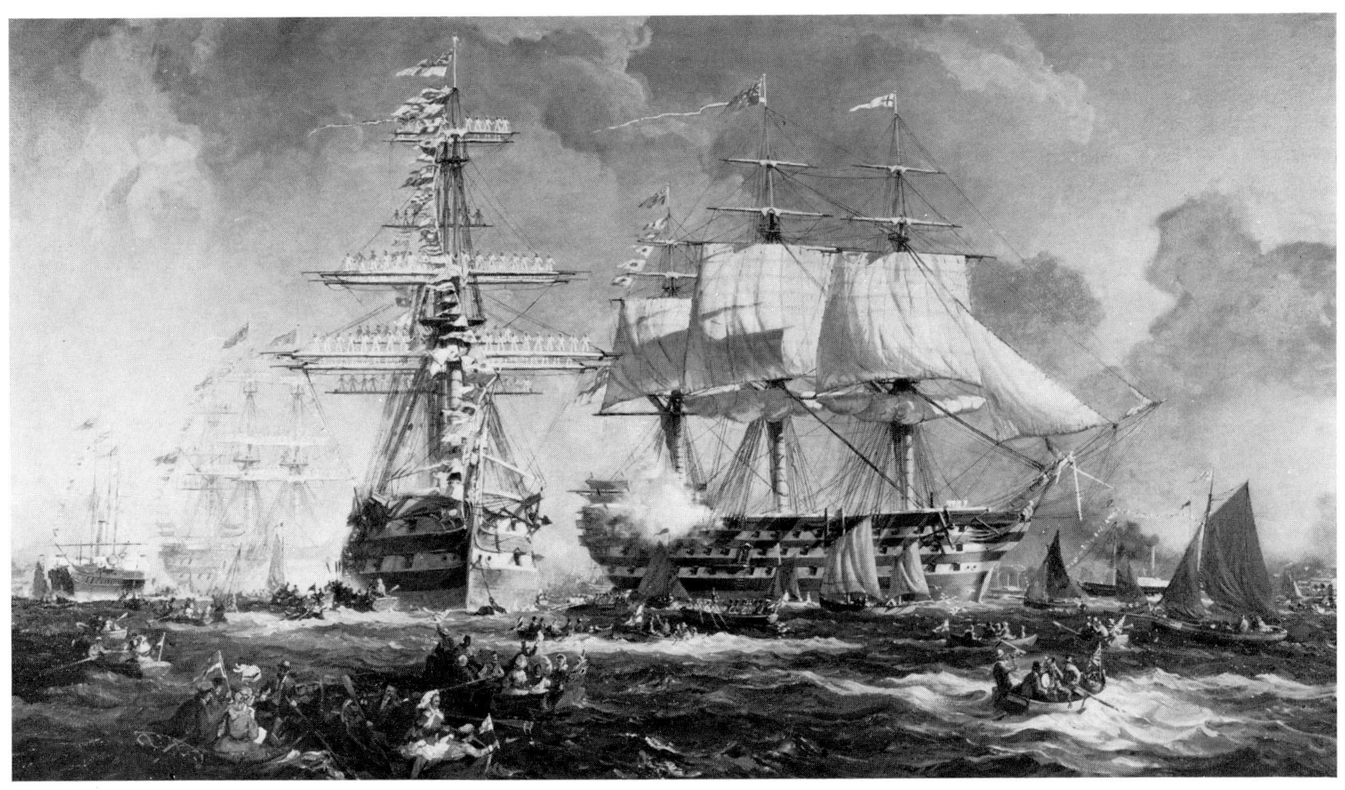

Cat. no. 115 H.R.H. THE PRINCE OF WALES LEAVING PLYMOUTH, 1861 Canvas, 60 x 114 ins.
In the possession of Liberty & Co. Ltd., London

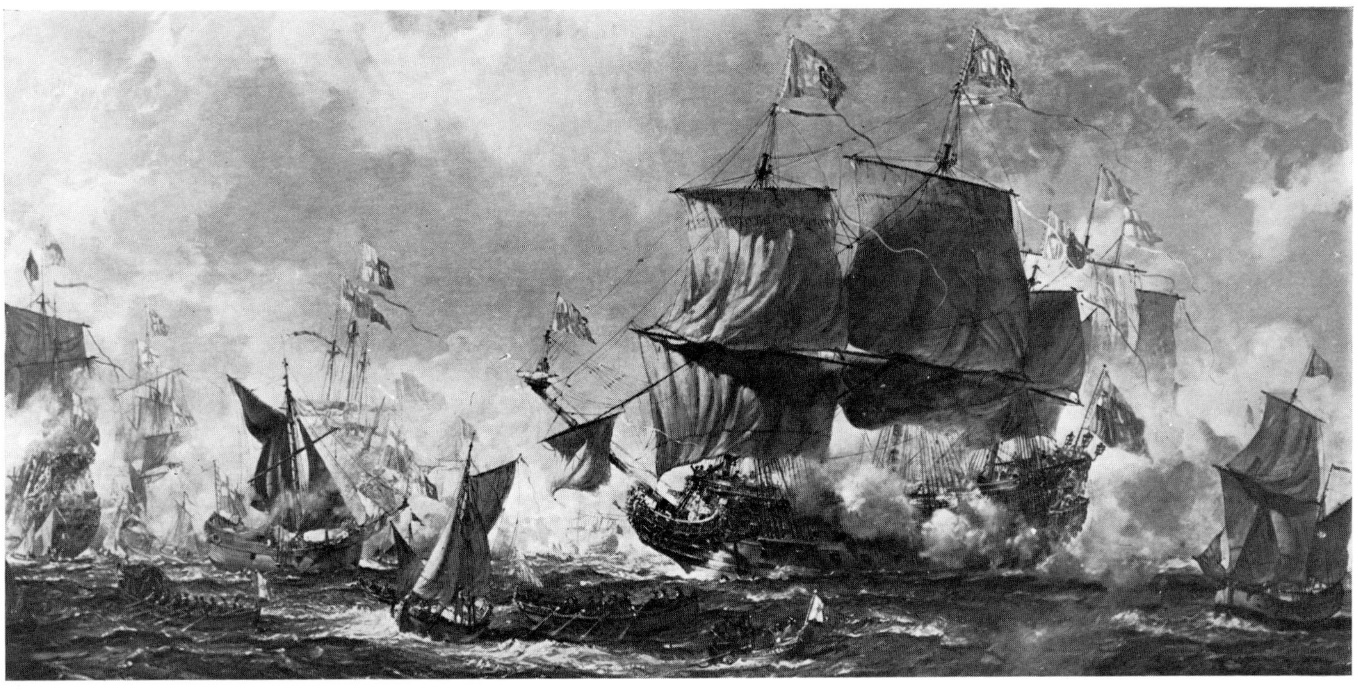

Cat. no. 116 MR. PEPYS' NAVY Canvas, 48 x 96 ins.
In the possession of Mr. J. Jervis

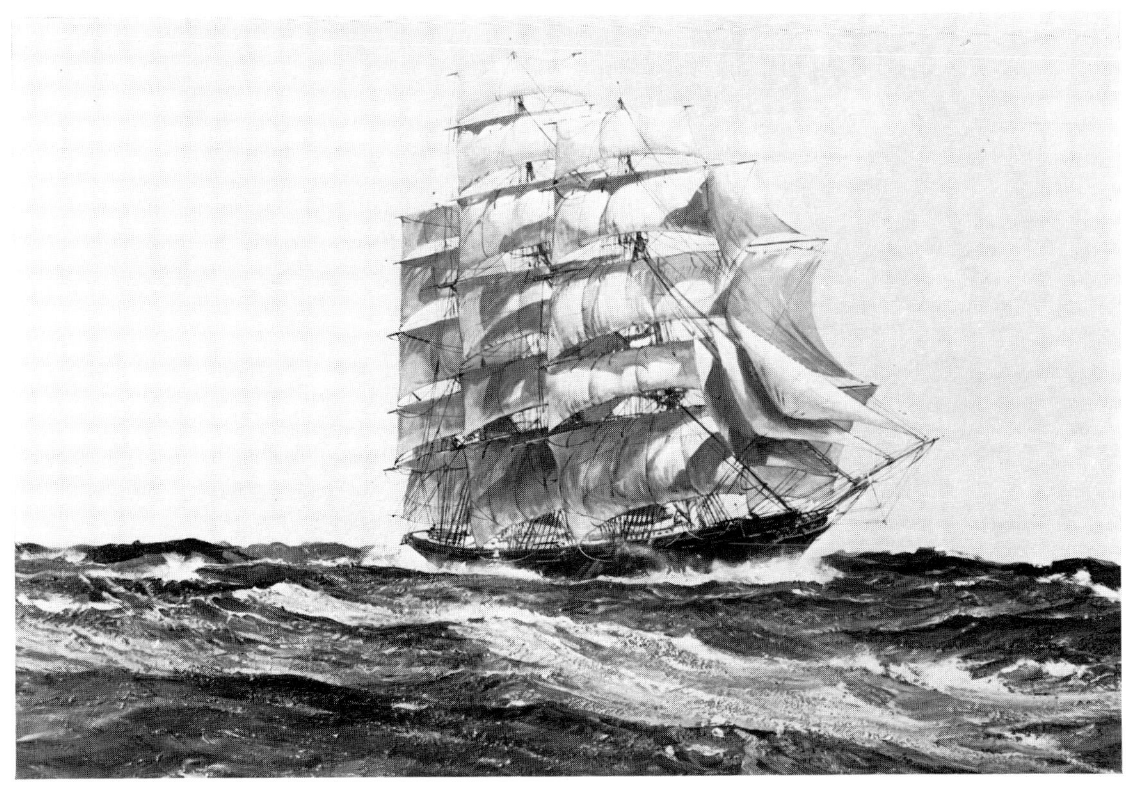

Cat. no. 122 CUTTY SARK Canvas, 20 x 30 ins.
In the possession of Mr. Lyman

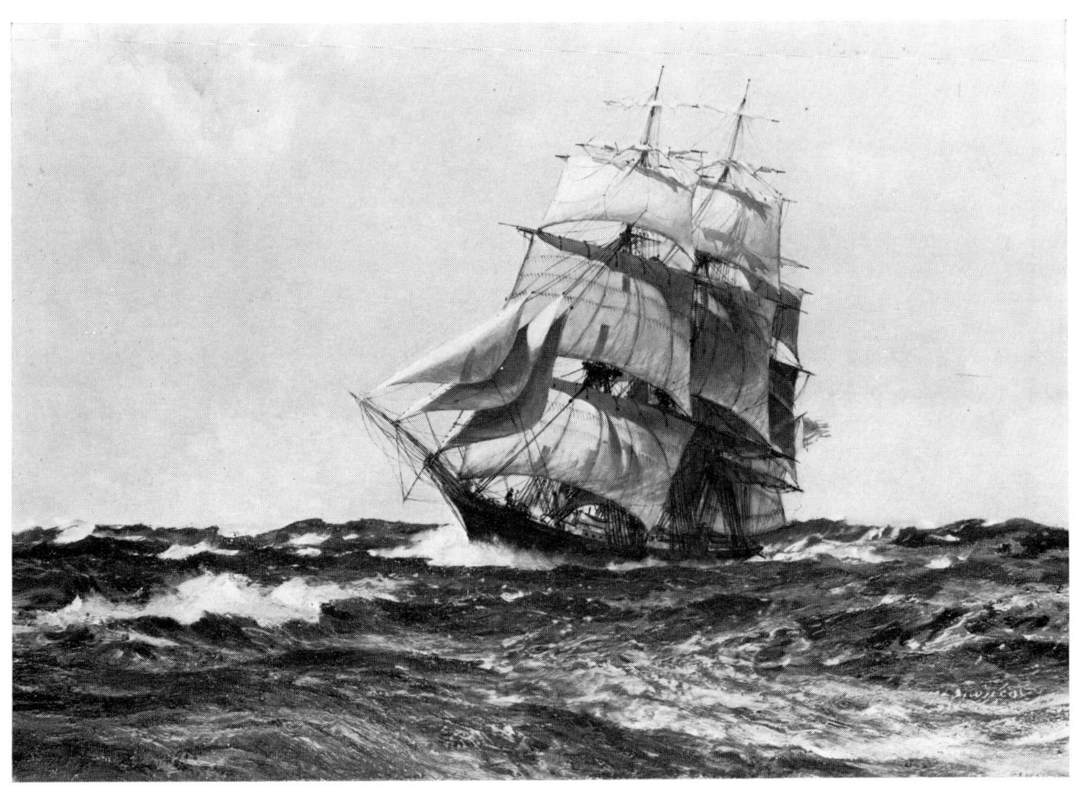

Cat. no. 128 THE U.S. CLIPPER 'YOUNG AMERICA' Canvas, 29 x 40 ins.

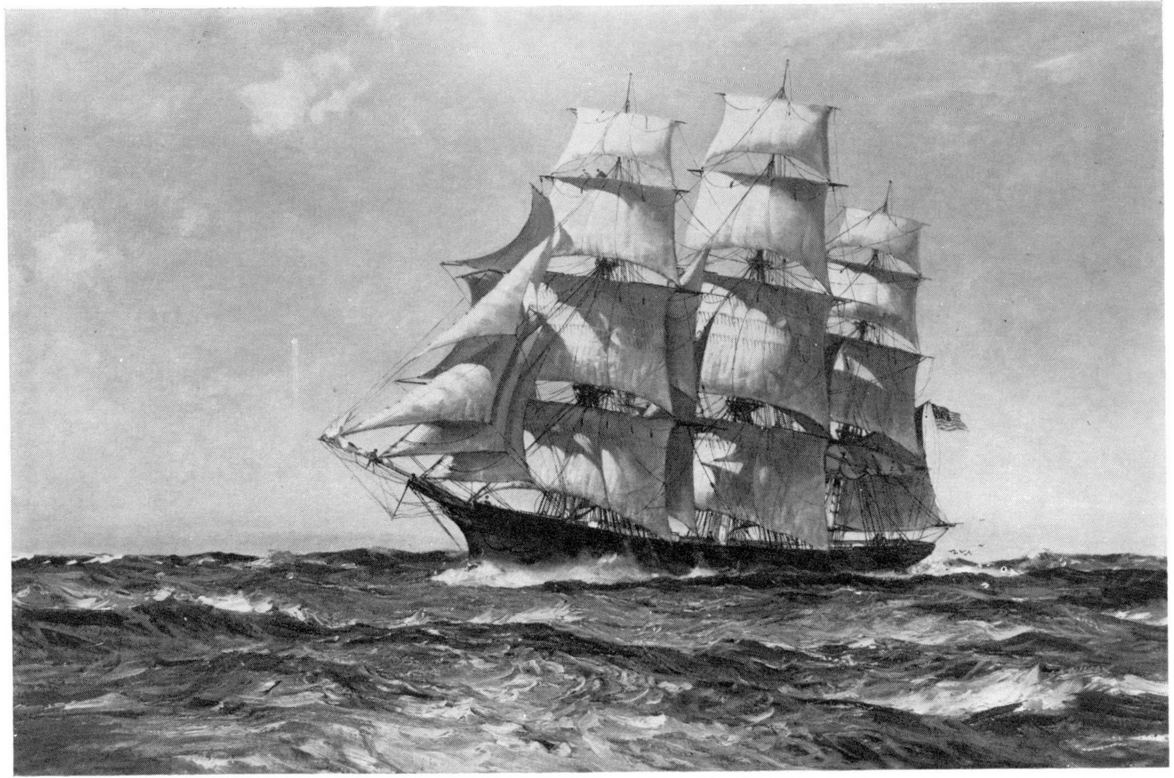

Cat. no. 134 THE UNITED STATES CLIPPER 'ARCHER' Canvas, 28 x 40 ins.

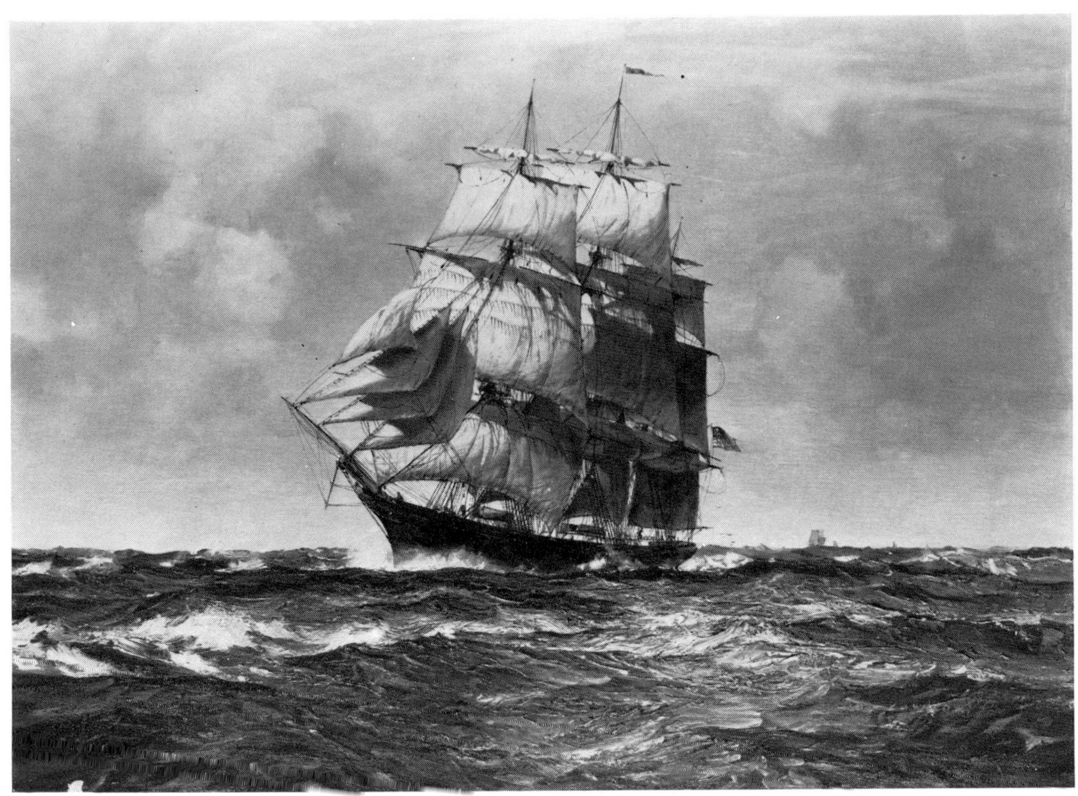

Cat. no. 137 THE UNITED STATES CLIPPER 'STARLIGHT' Canvas, 28 x 40 ins.

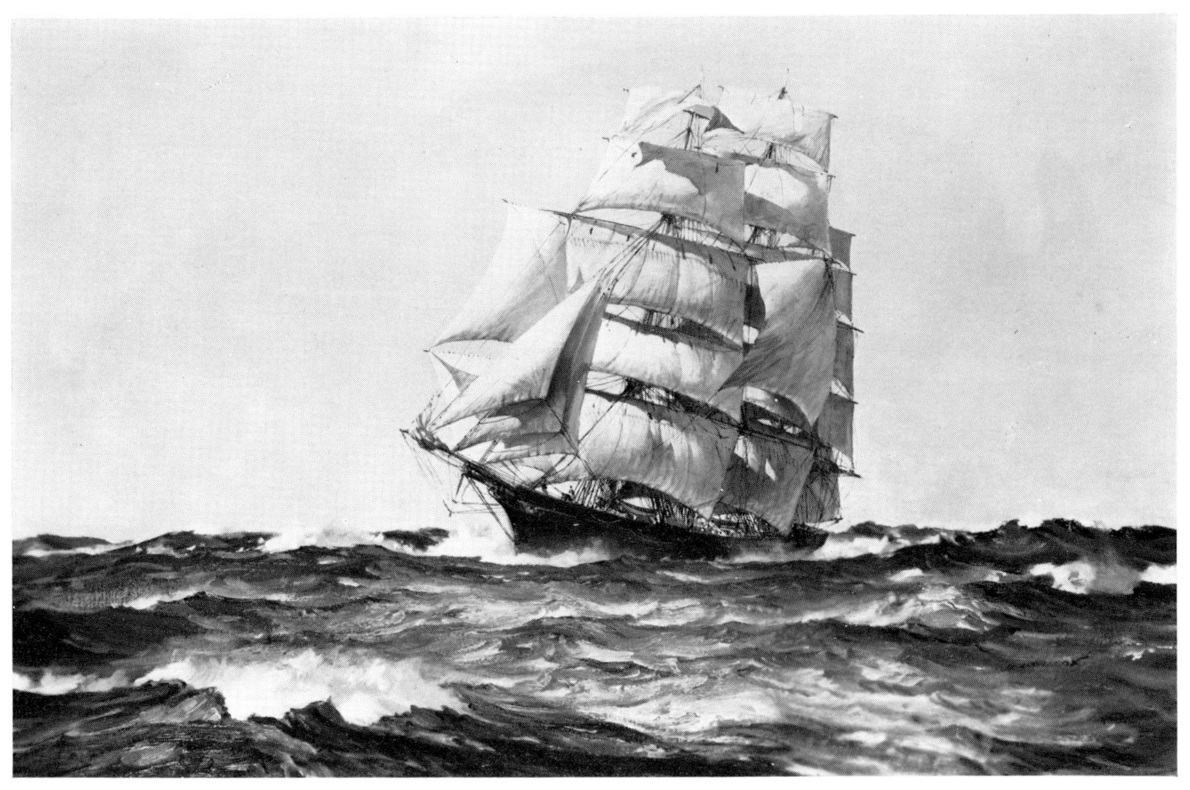

Cat. no. 138 THE UNITED STATES CLIPPER 'PRIMA DONNA' Canvas, 25 x 40 ins.

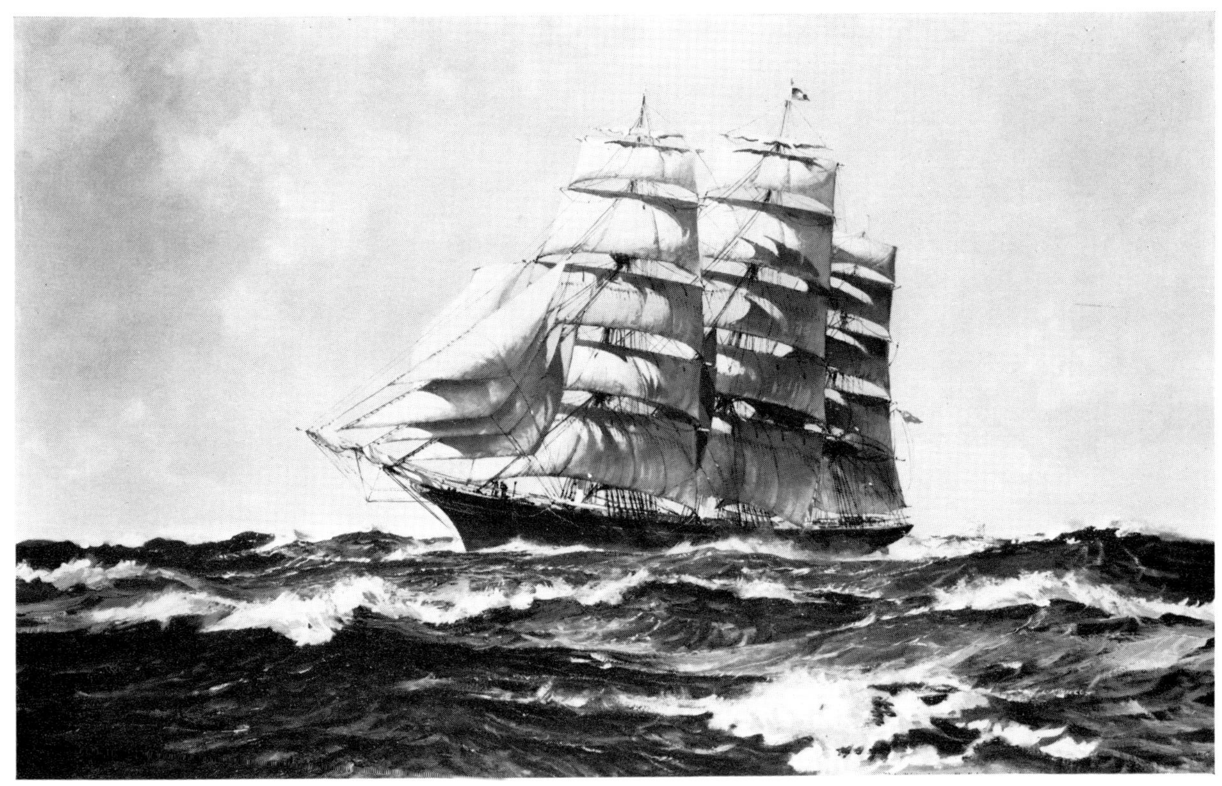

Cat. no. 139 THE 'THERMOPYLAE' Canvas, 28 x 30 ins.

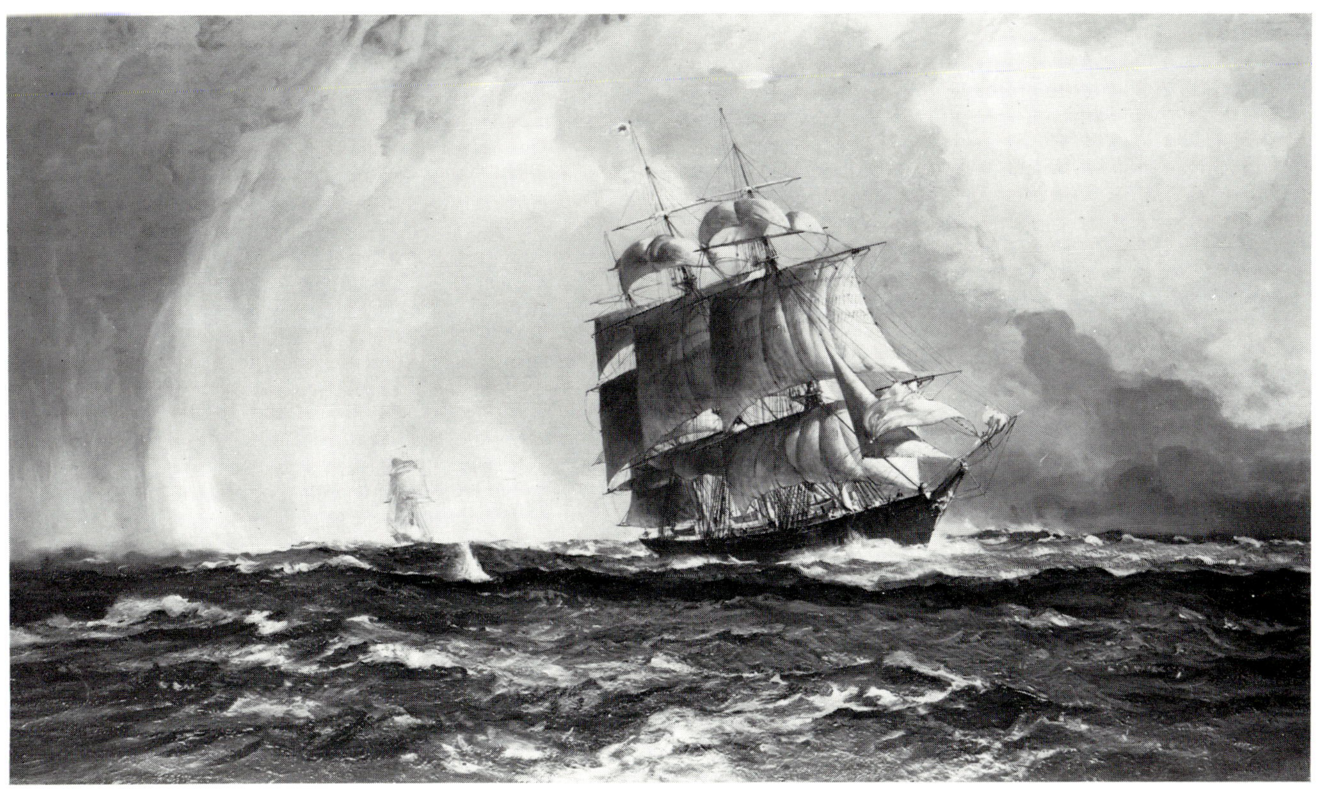

Cat. no. 143 THE CRUISER 'ALABAMA' & THE CLIPPER 'WINGED RACER' Canvas, 36 x 60 ins.

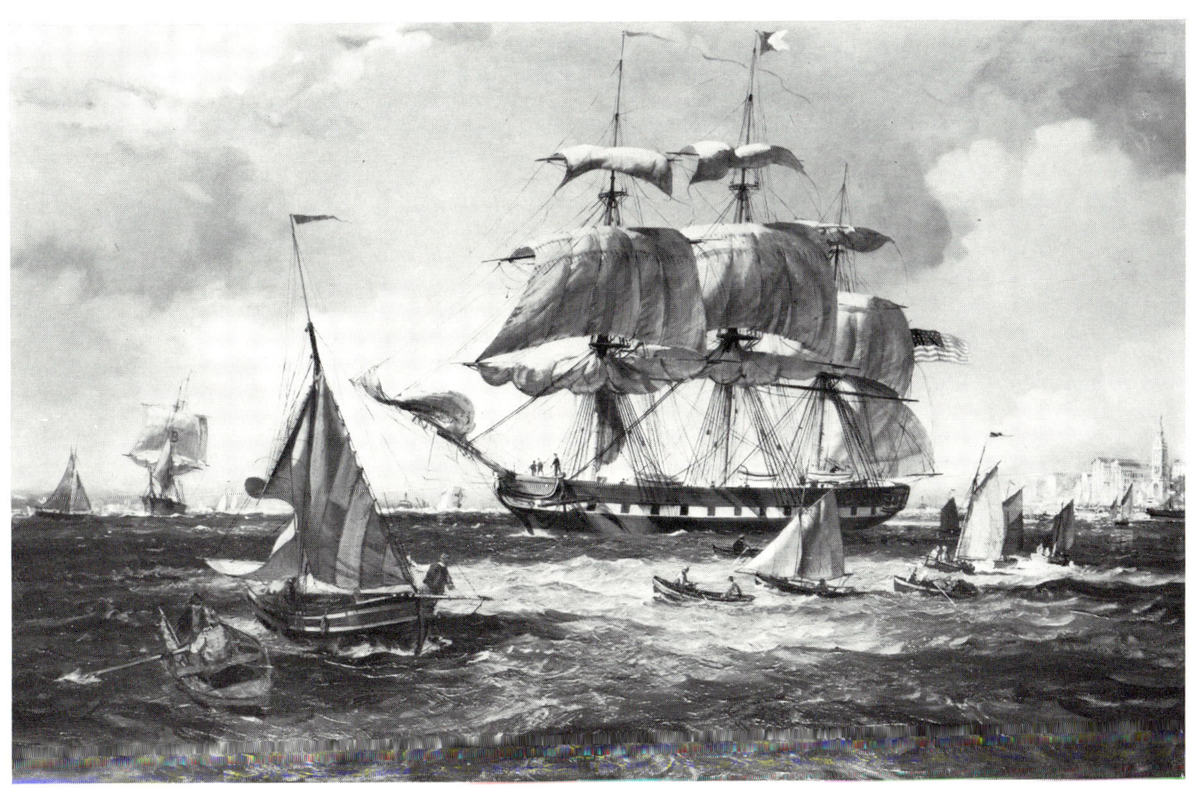

Cat. no. 110 CHARLES DICKENS LEAVING LIVERPOOL IN THE PACKET 'GEORGE WASHINGTON' Canvas, 40 x 60 ins.

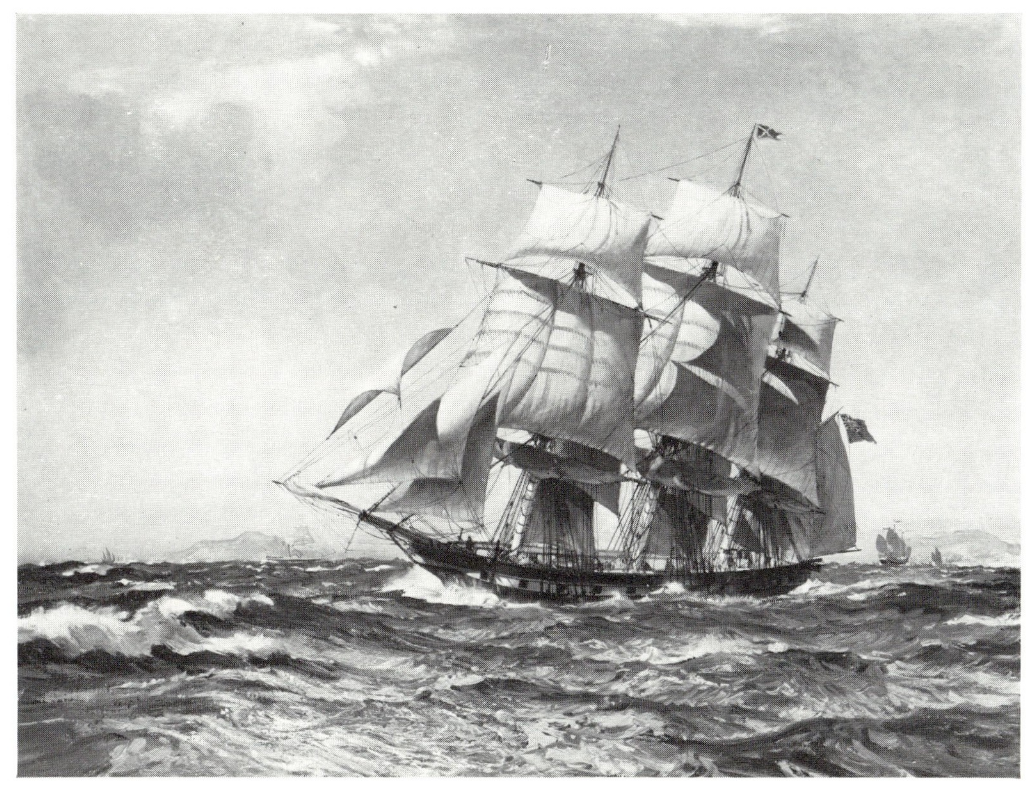

Cat. no.151 THE OPIUM CLIPPER 'FALCON' Canvas, 28 x 36 ins.

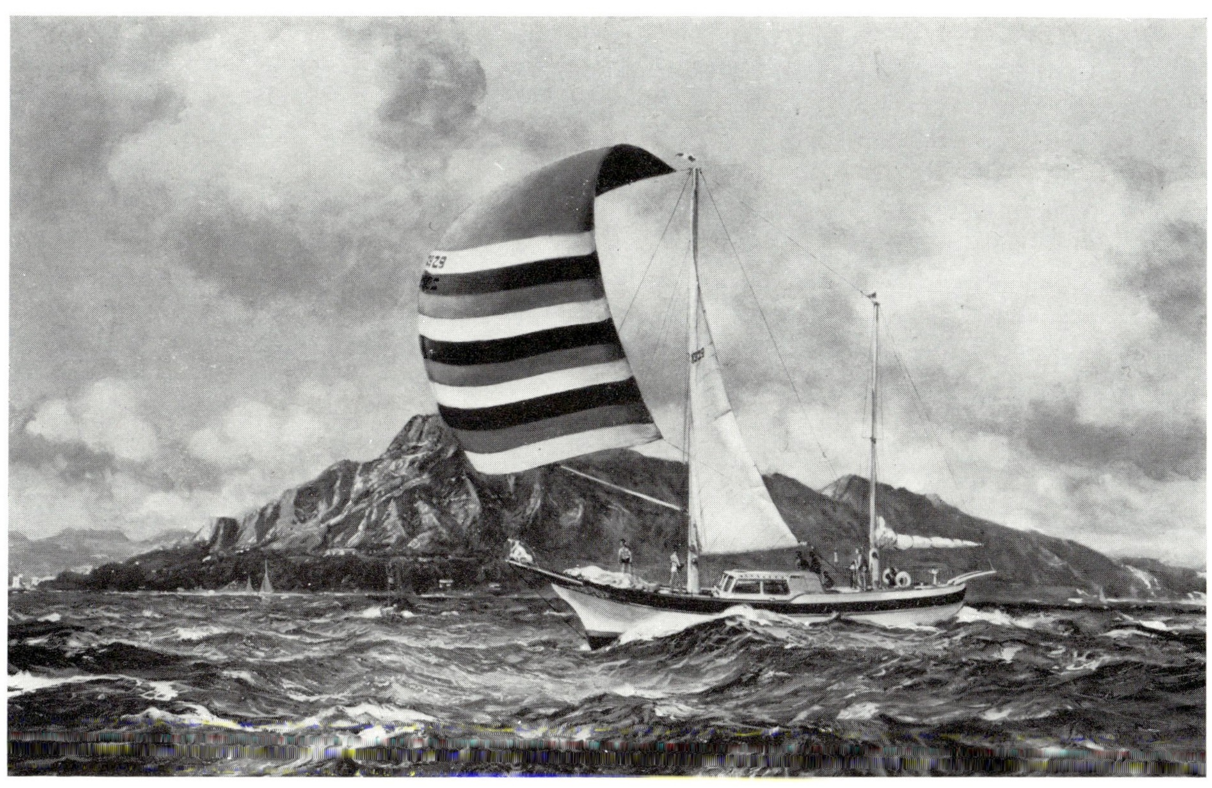

Cat. no. 153 THE YACHT 'MYSTIC' OFF DIAMOND ROCK, HAWAII Canvas, 30 x 40 ins.
In the possession of Mr. Marvyn Carton

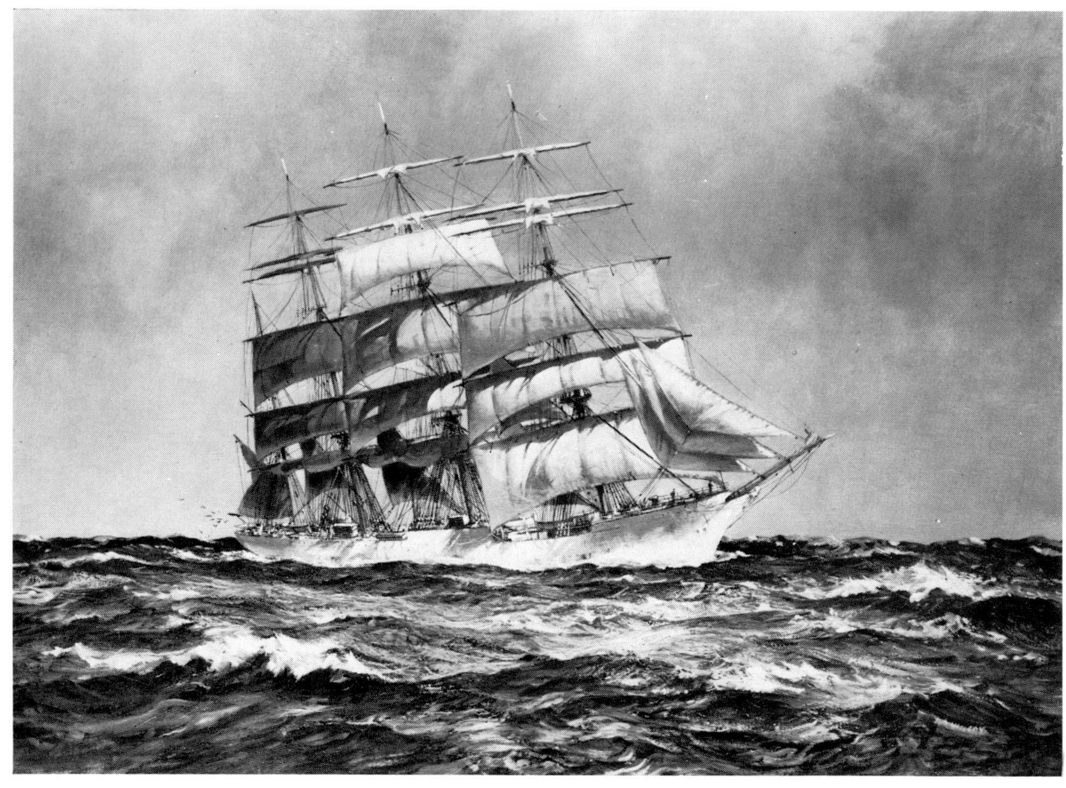

Cat. no. 155 THE 'HERTZOGIN CECILE' Canvas, 30 x 40 ins.

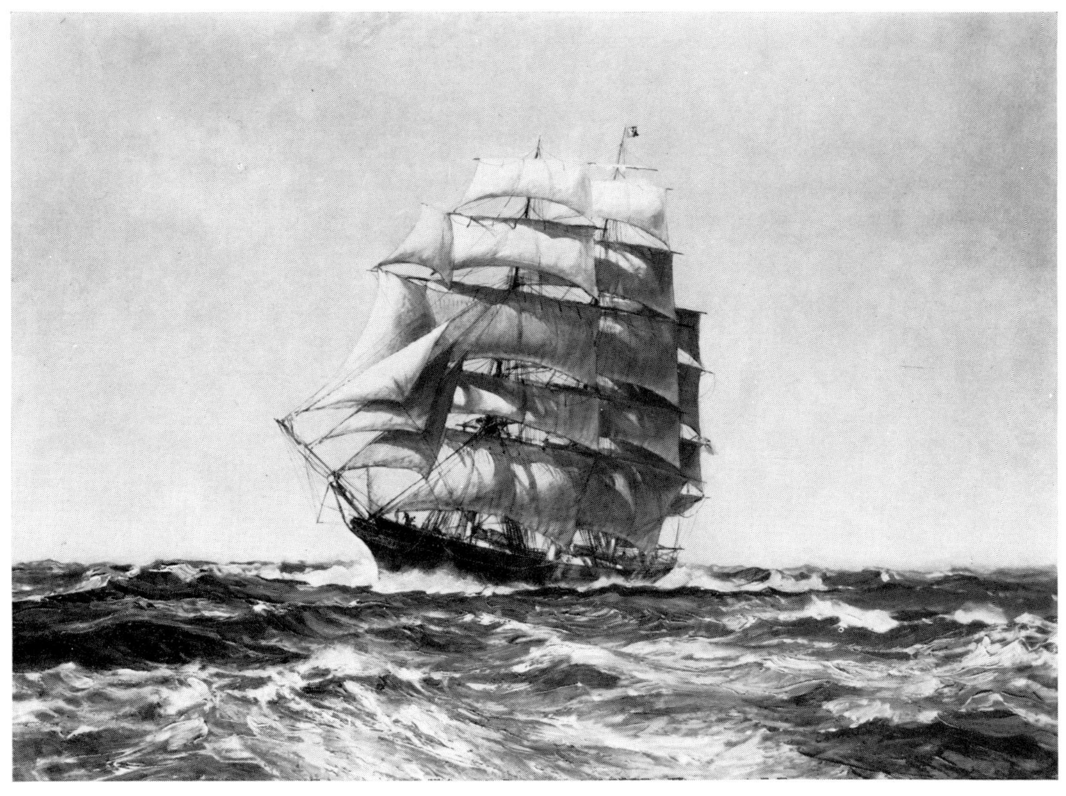

Cat. no. 156 THE 'NORMAN COURT' Canvas, 28 x 40 ins.

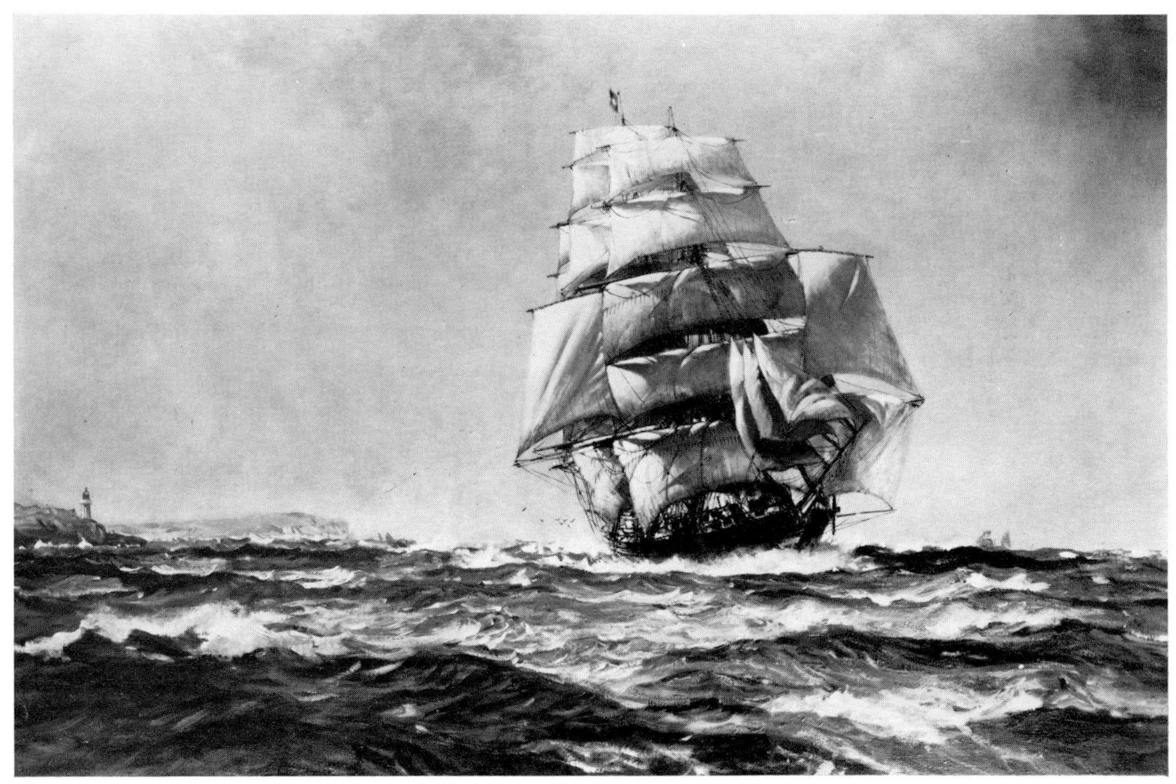

Cat. no. 157 THE CLIPPER 'SOUTH AUSTRALIAN' Canvas, 30 x 45 ins.

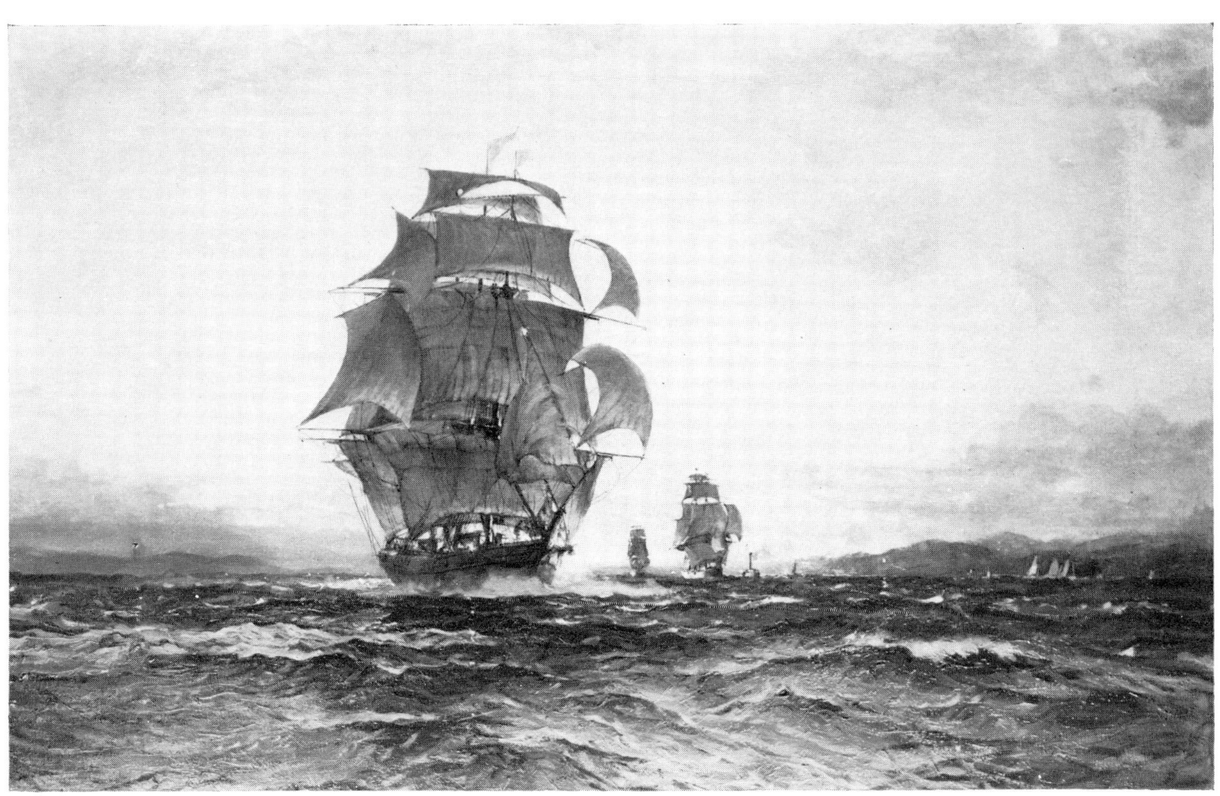

Cat. no. 158 CLIPPERS 'METEOR, 'GAMECOCK' & 'TELEGRAPH' AT GOLDEN GATE Canvas, 30 x 46 ins.

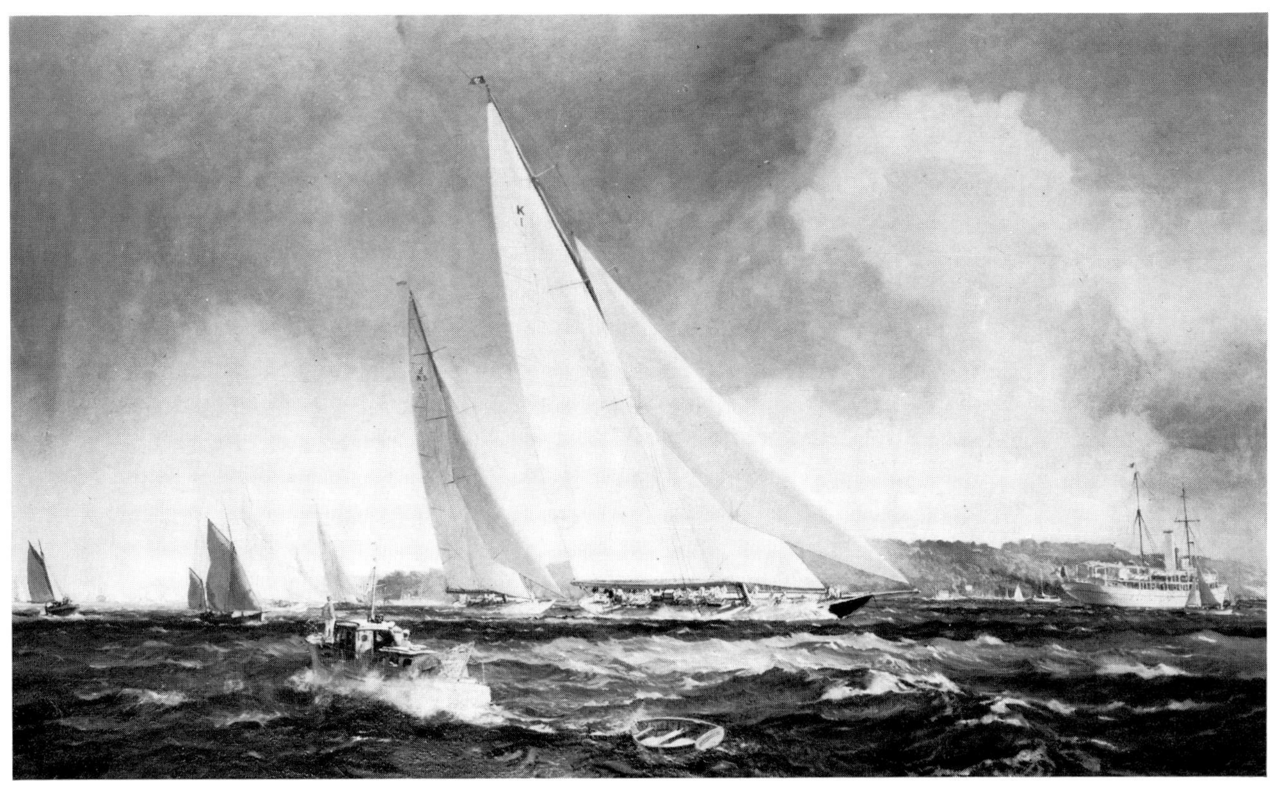

Cat. no. 162 THE ROYAL YACHT 'BRITANNIA' RACING IN THE SOLENT Canvas, 40 x 60 ins.
In the possession of Dr Beppé Croce

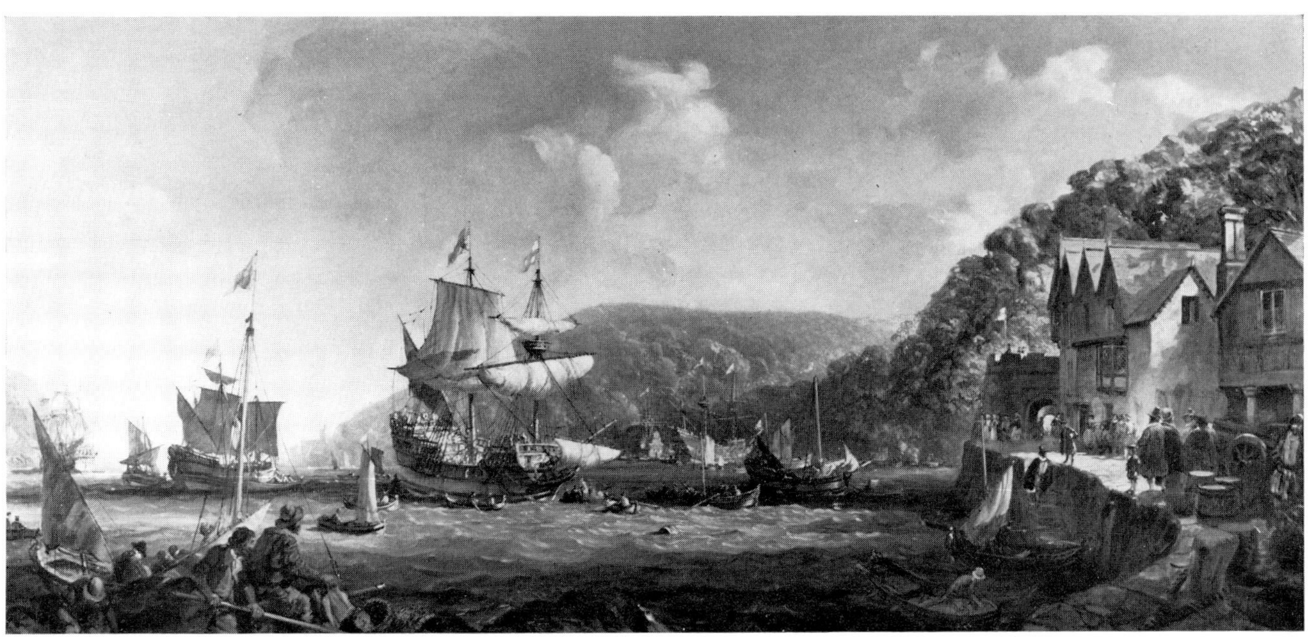

Cat. no. 163 THE 'MAYFLOWER' & 'SPEEDWELL' AT DARTMOUTH Canvas, 42 x 84 ins.
In the possession of the Pilgrim Society, Plymouth, Massachusetts, U.S.A.

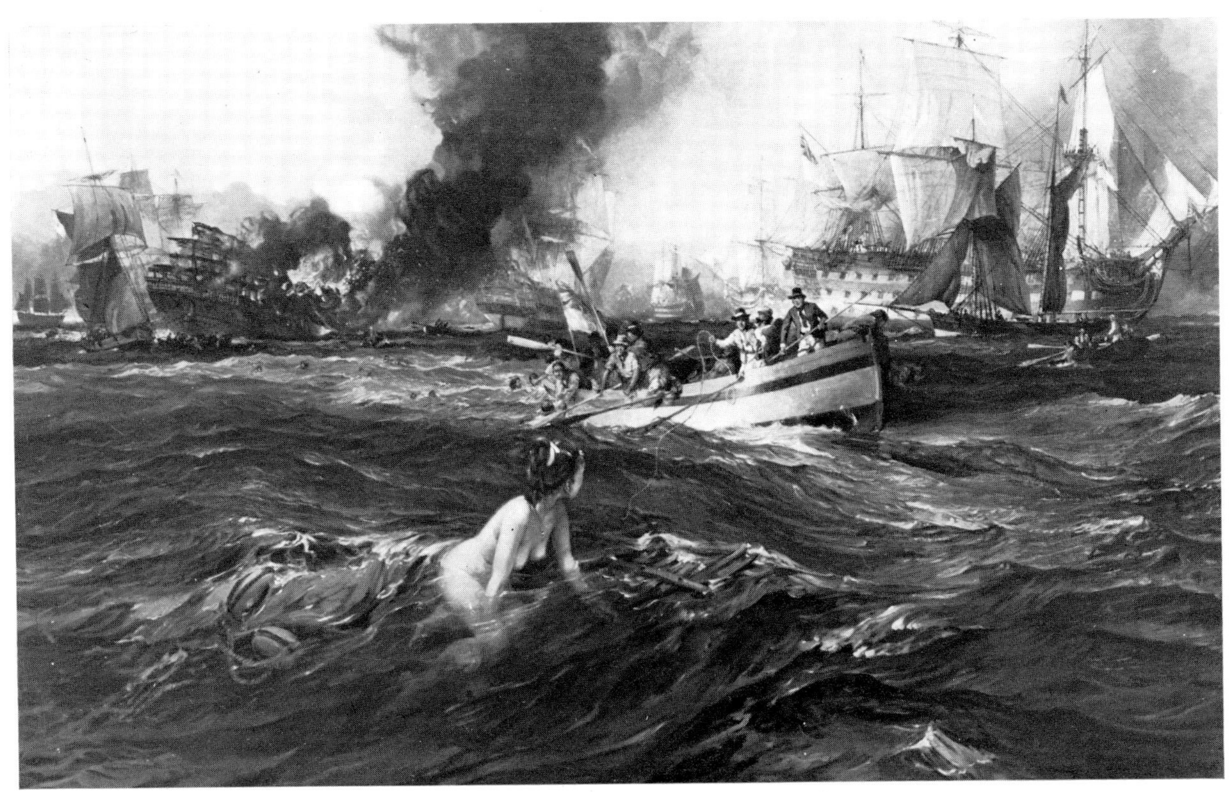

Cat. no. 164 'JEANNETTE' – BATTLE OF TRAFALGAR, 1805 Canvas, 40 x 60 ins.
In the possession of Mr. Garfield Weston

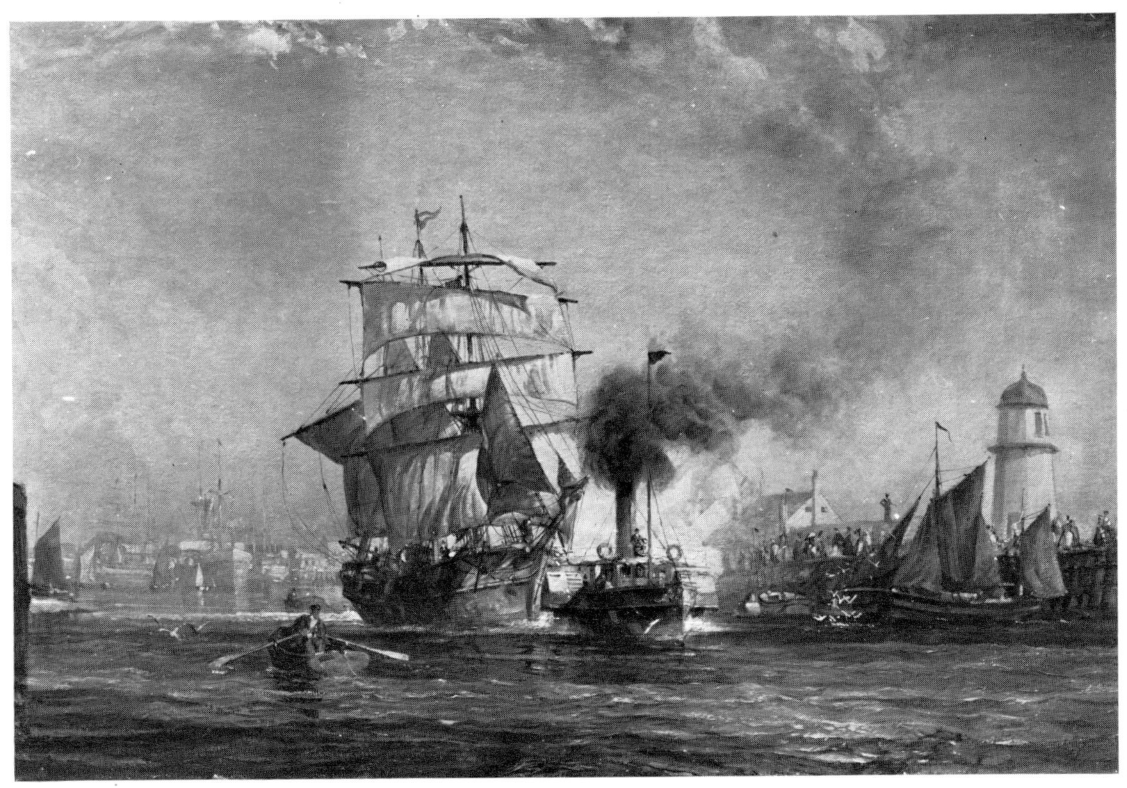

Cat. no.165 BARQUE TOWING OUT OF LITTLEHAMPTON Canvas, 30 x 45 ins.

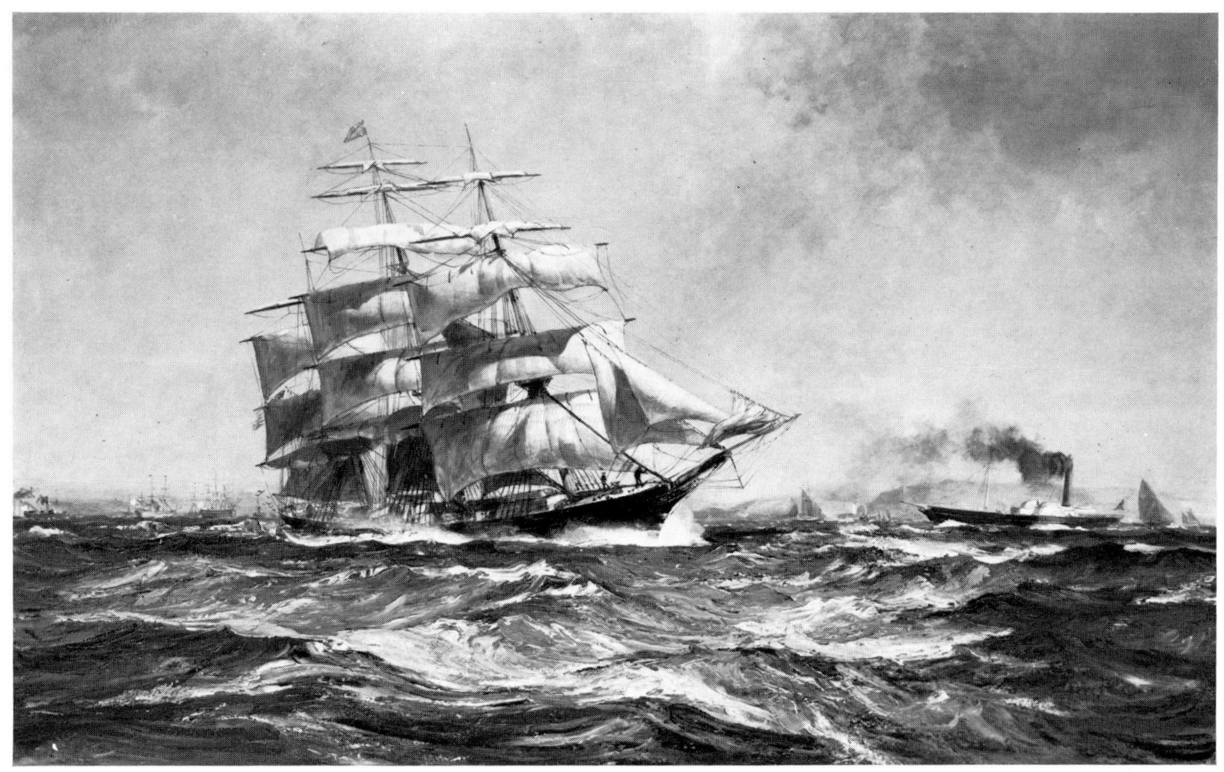

Cat. no. 166 U.S.A. CLIPPER 'RAVEN' LEAVING FALMOUTH Canvas, 30 x 45 ins.

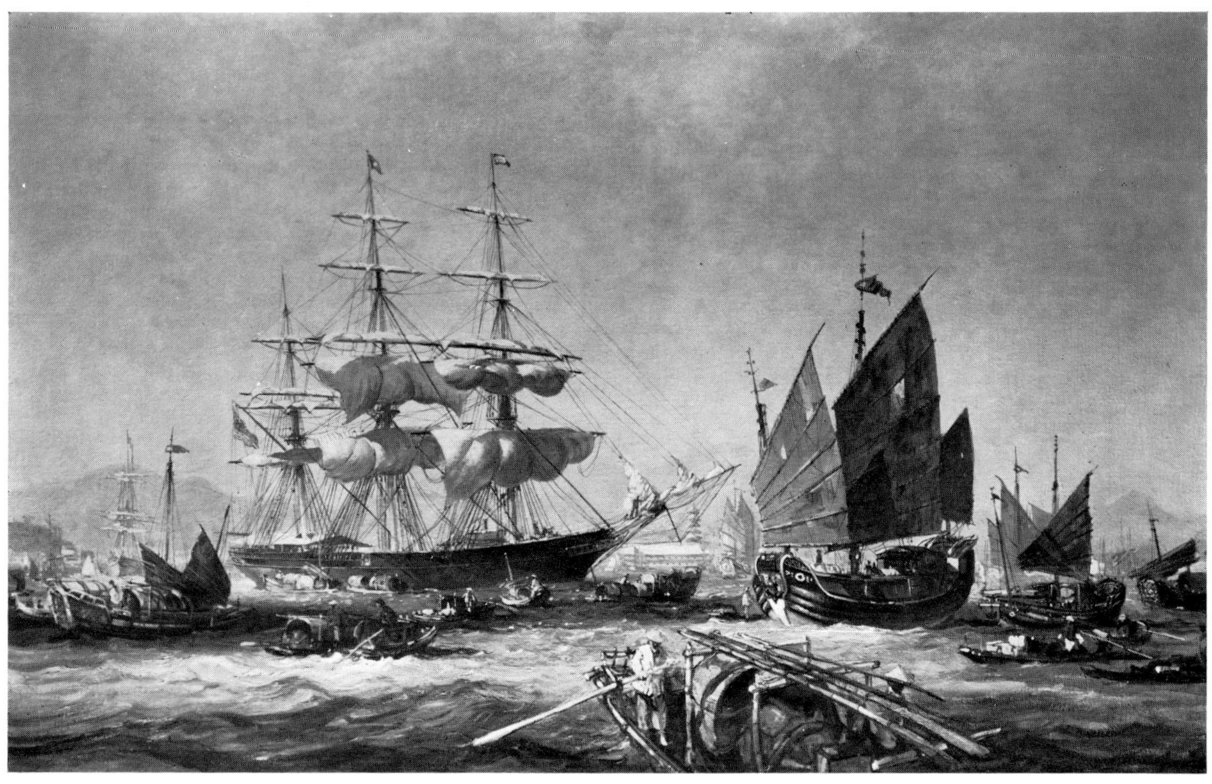

Cat. no. 167 U.S.A. CLIPPER 'RINGLEADER' AT FOOCHOW Canvas, 30 x 45 ins.

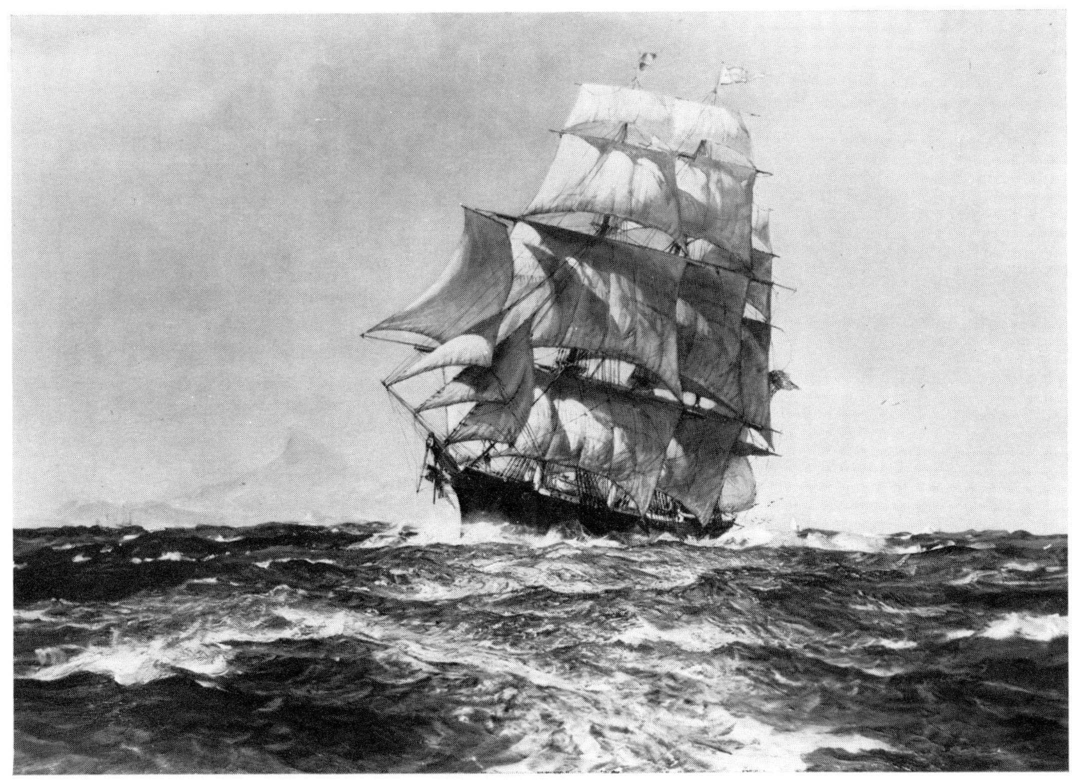

Cat. no. 173 THE CLIPPER 'FLYING EAGLE' Canvas, 30 x 40 ins.

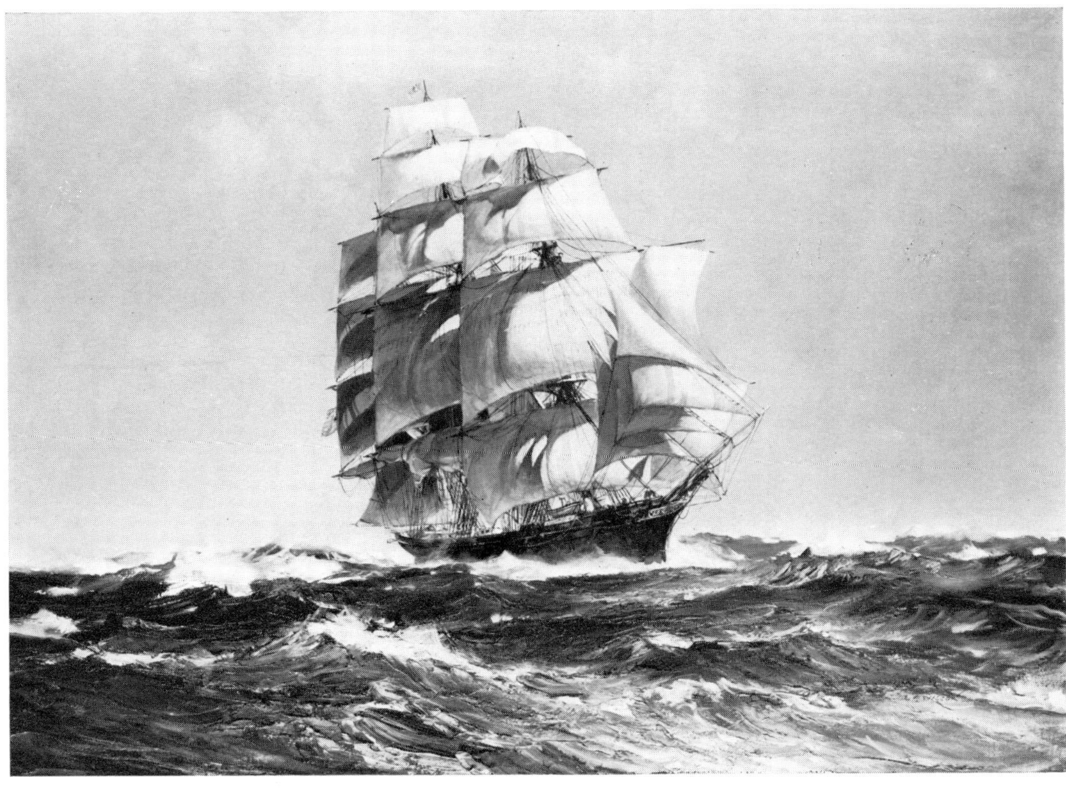

Cat. no. 174 THE CLIPPER 'GOLDEN EAGLE' Canvas, 30 x 40 ins.

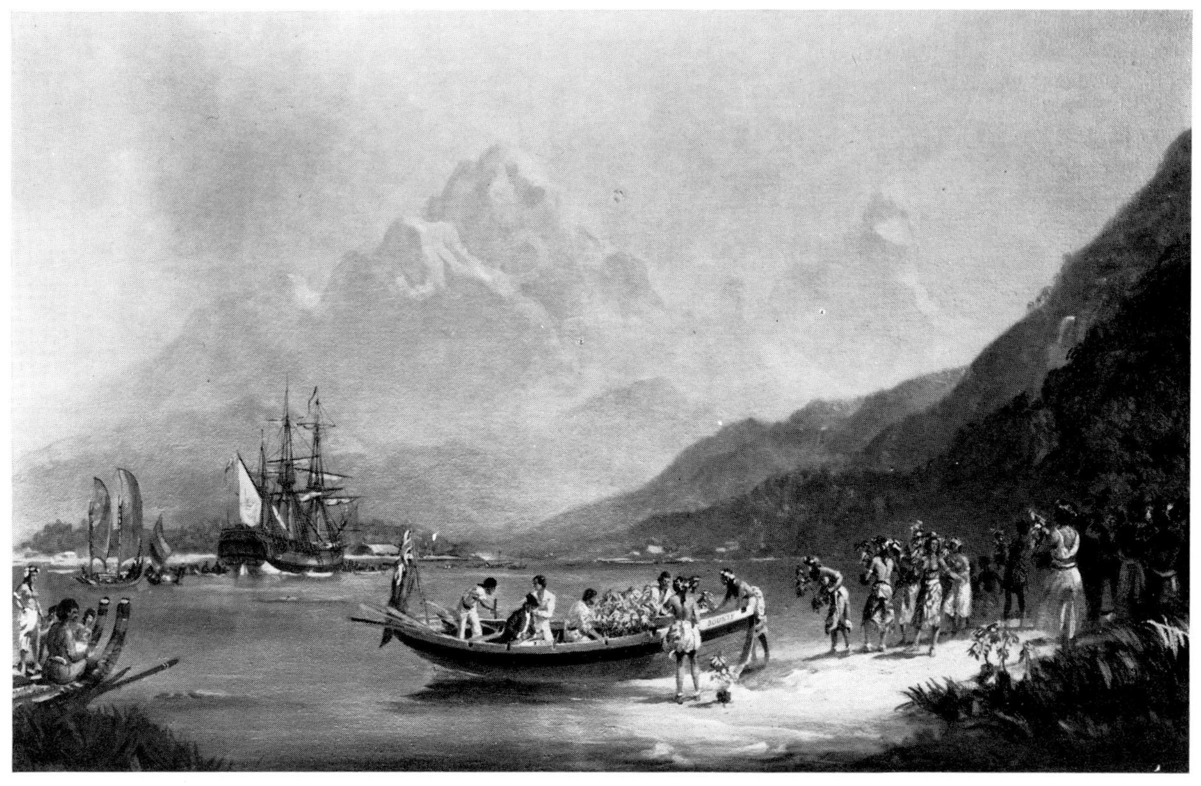

Cat. no. 175 THE 'BOUNTY' AT MATAVIA BAY, TAHITI, 1789 Canvas, 25 x 40 ins.

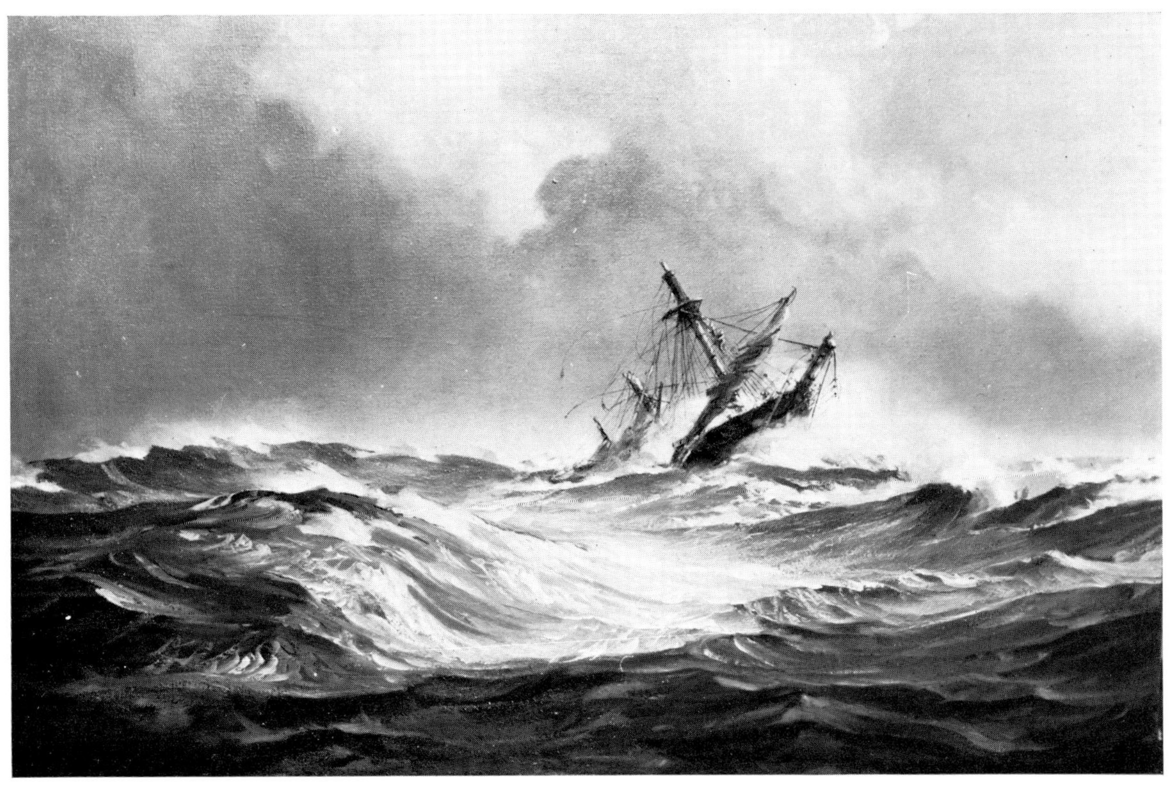

Cat. no. 176 SHIPWRECK Canvas, 27 x 40 ins.

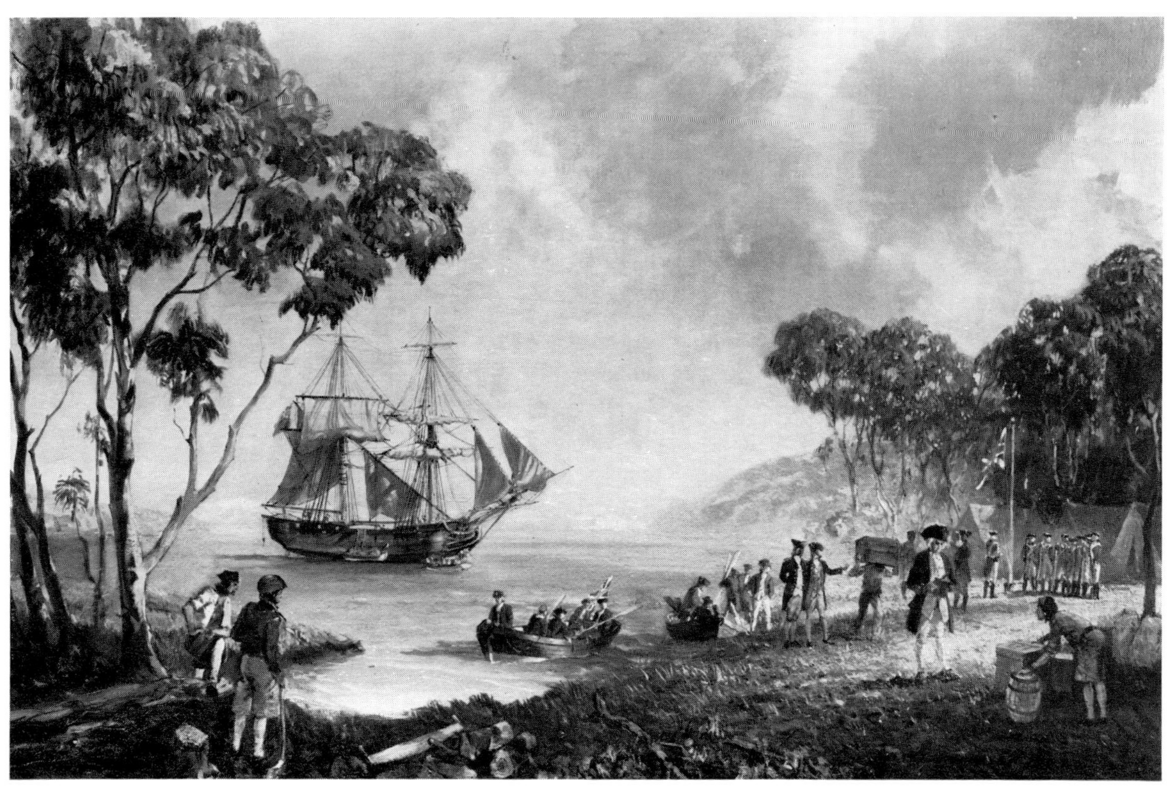

Cat. no. 177 CAPTAIN PHILLIPS LANDING AT SIDNEY COVE Canvas, 25 x 40 ins.
In a private Australian collection

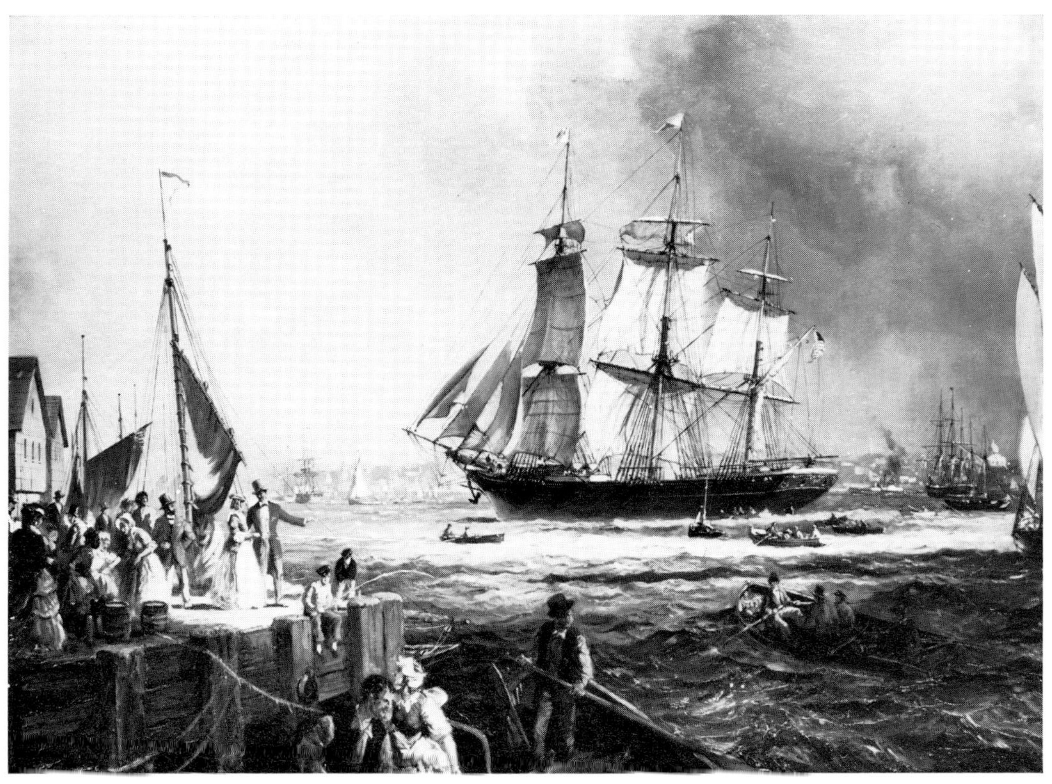

Cat. no. 179 THE 'JOHN GILPIN' AT BOSTON Canvas, 40 x 60 ins.

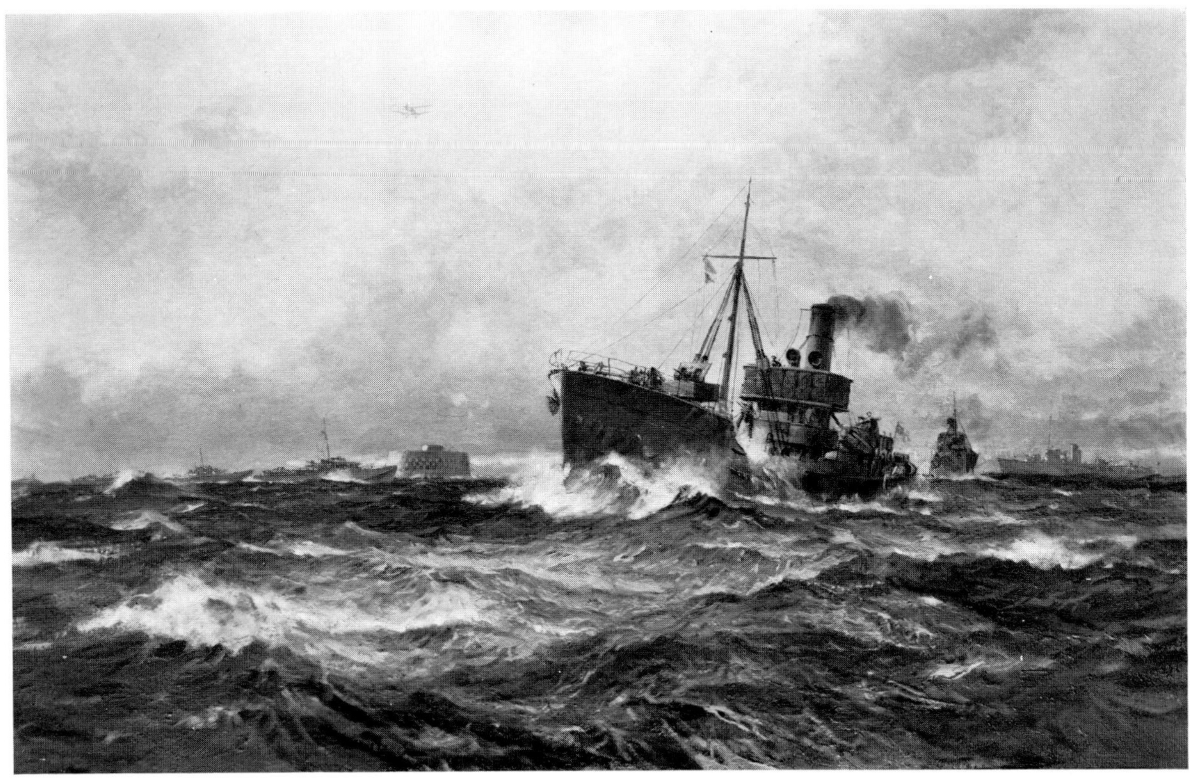

Cat. no. 180 R.N.V.R. TRAWLER OFF PORTSMOUTH Canvas, 30 x 45 ins.

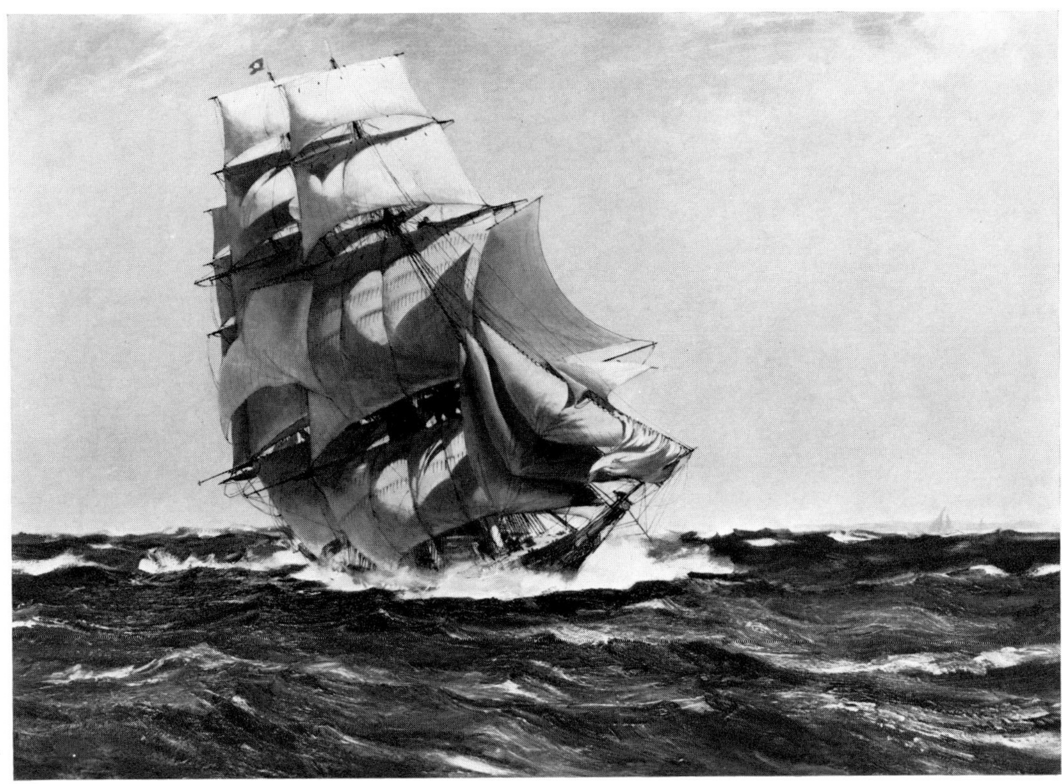

Cat. no. 184 THE CLIPPER 'RED JACKET' Canvas, 30 x 40 ins.

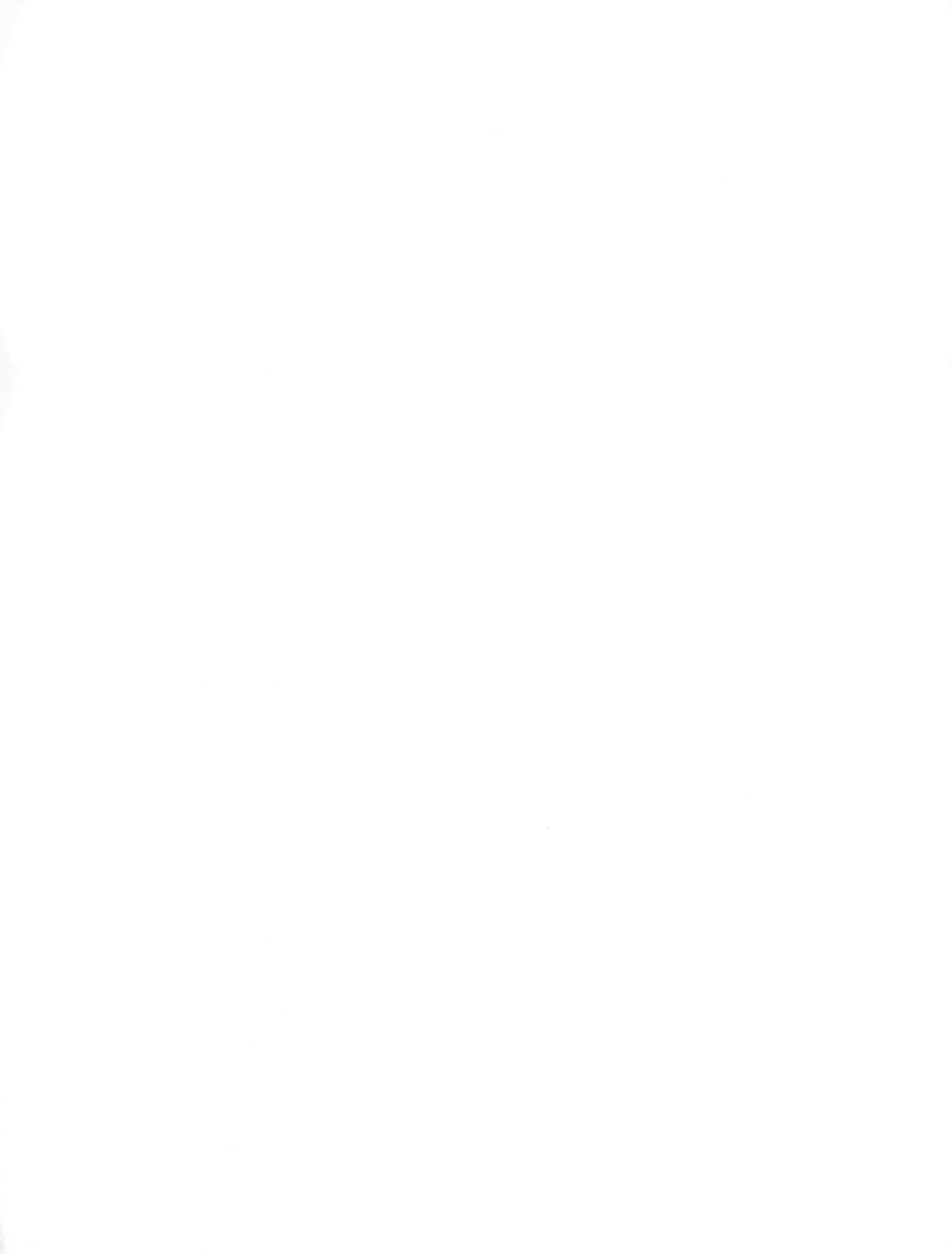

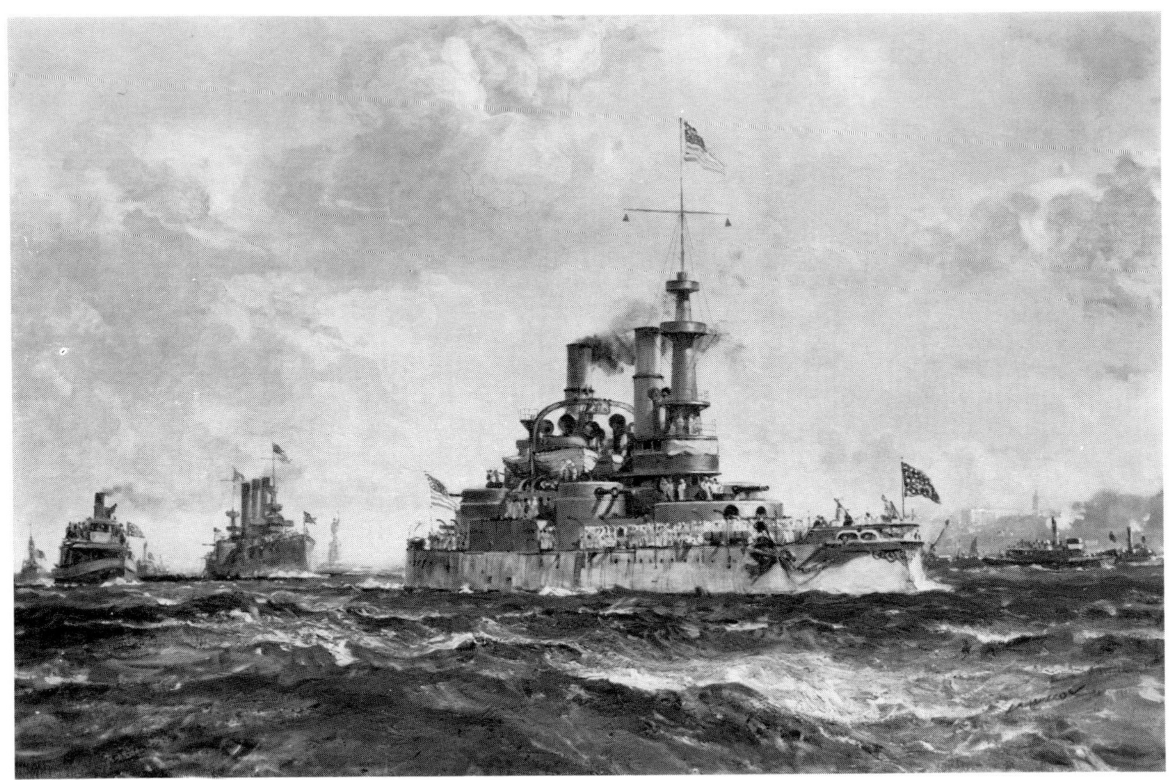

Cat. no. 191 THE U.S. FLEET RETURNING TO NEW YORK AFTER THE SPANISH-AMERICAN WAR Canvas, 24 x 36 ins.

In the possession of Mr. W. Cramp Scheetz, Junior

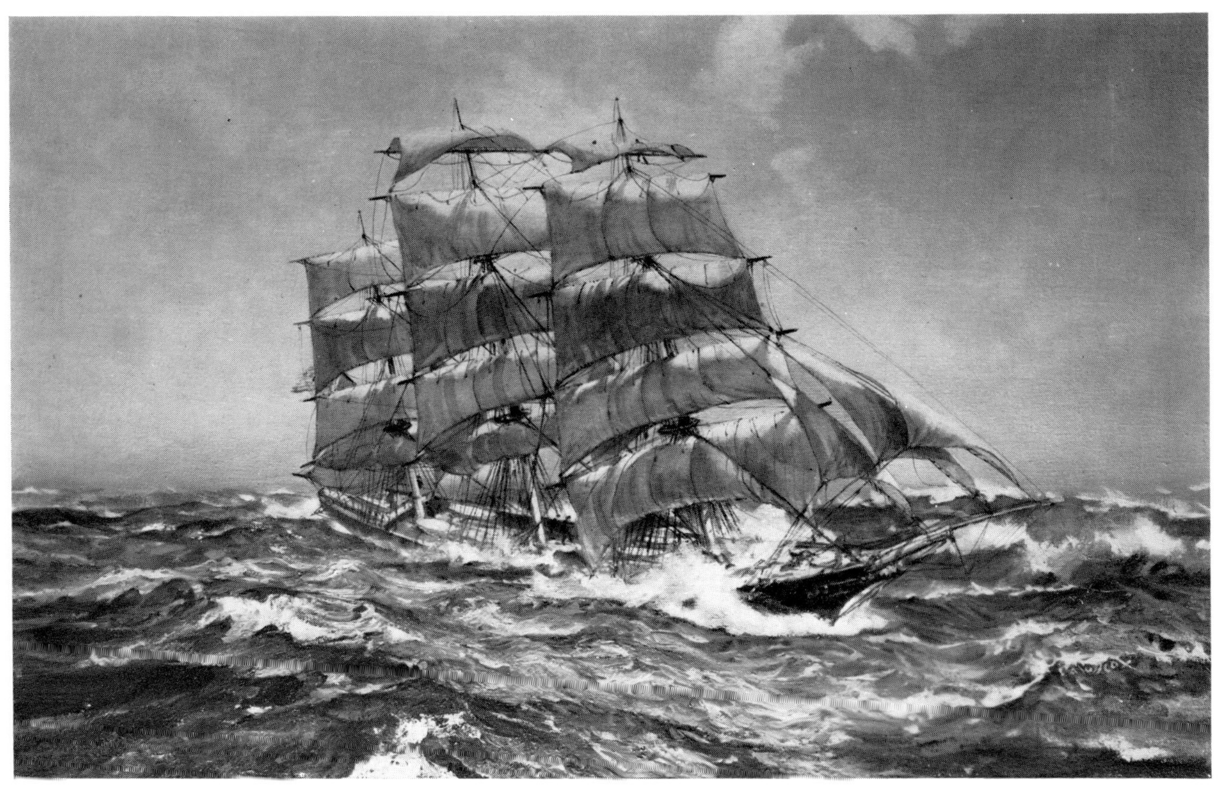

Cat. no. 193 U.S. CLIPPER 'OCEAN ROVER' Canvas, 24 x 36 ins.

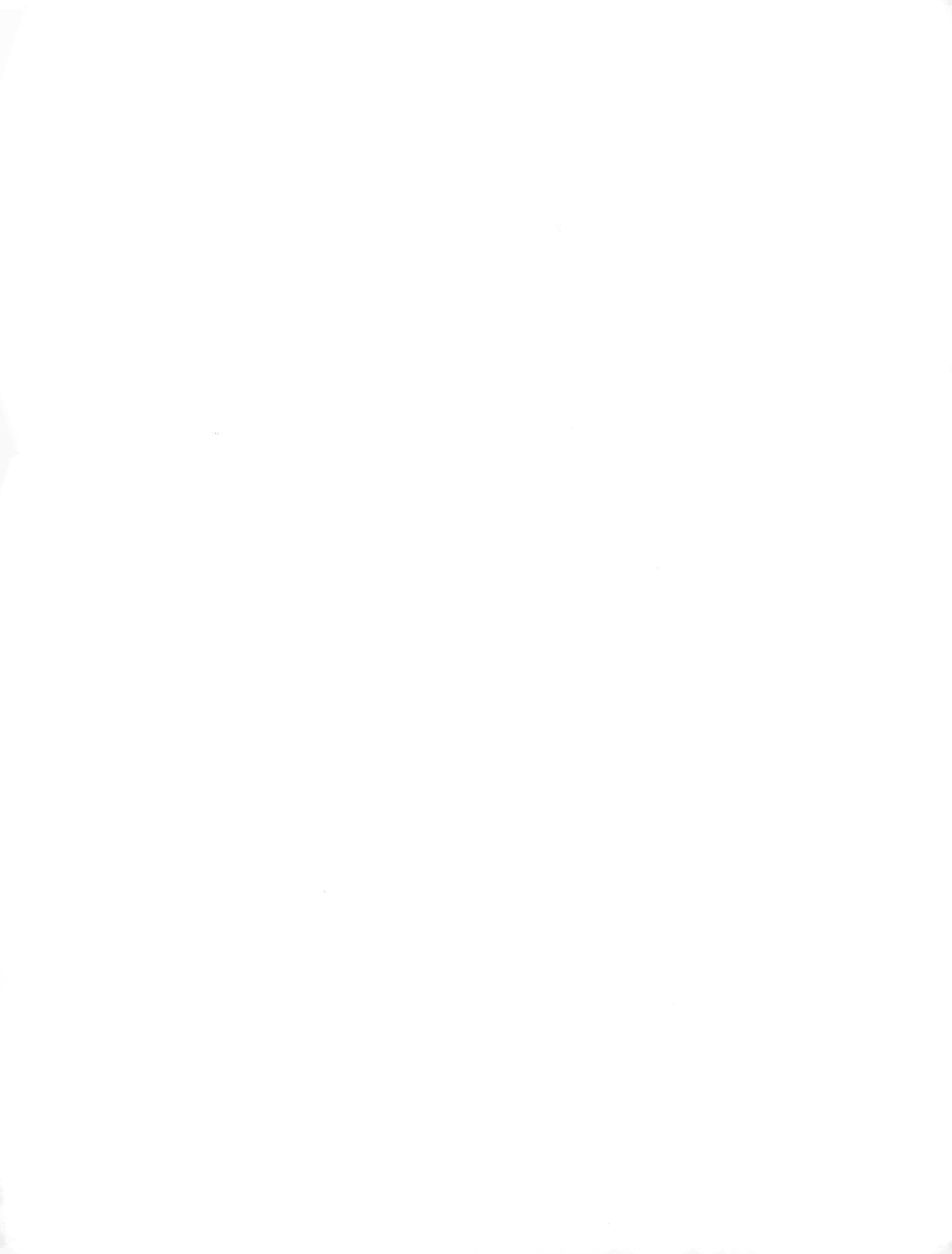

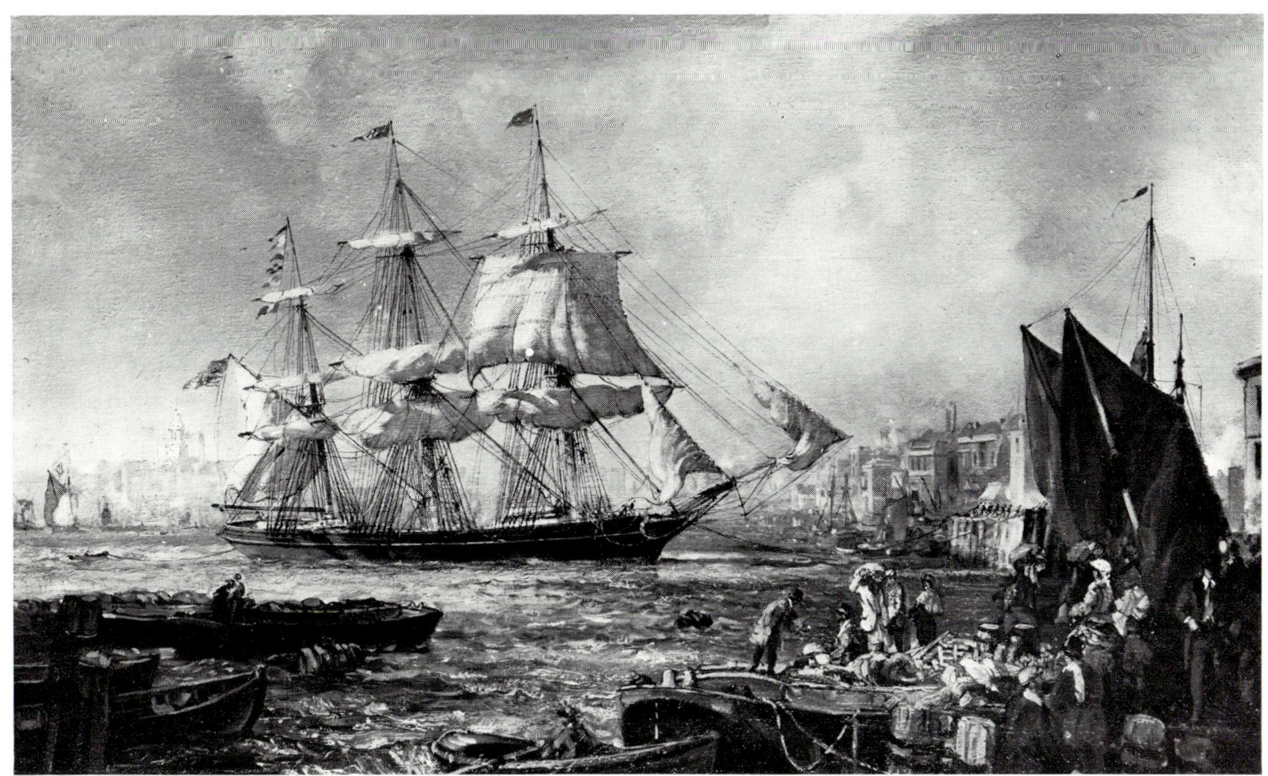

Cat. no. 195 U.S. CLIPPER 'ORIENTAL' AT LIMEHOUSE Canvas, 27 x 40 ins.

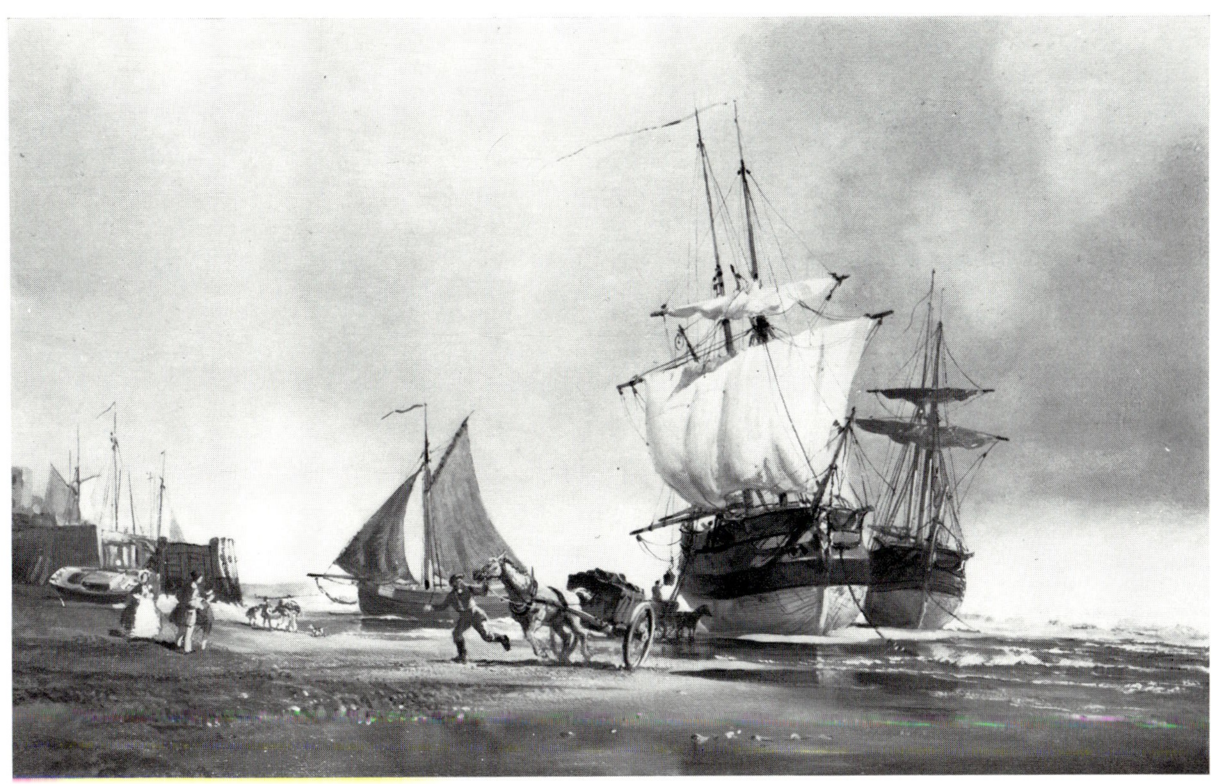

Cat. no. 197 BRIGHTON BEACH, *c.* 1850 Canvas, 20 x 30 ins.

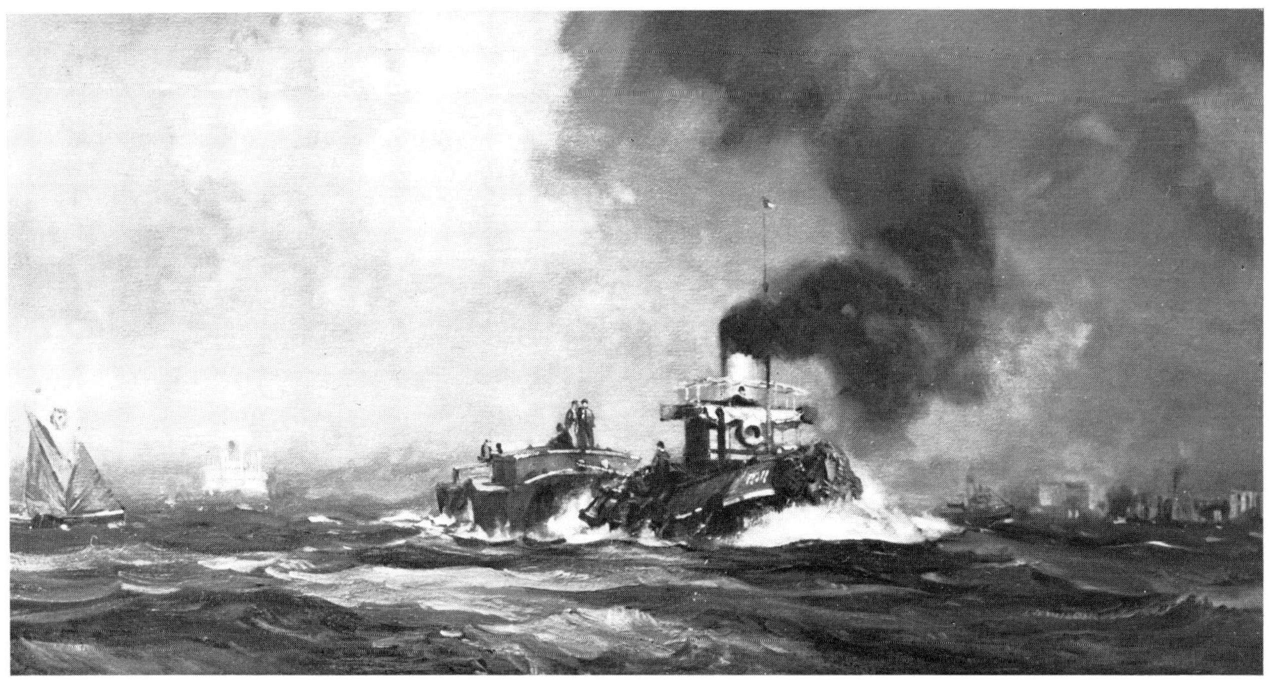

Cat. no. 198 HIGH WATER AT GRAVESEND Canvas, 19 x 13 ins.

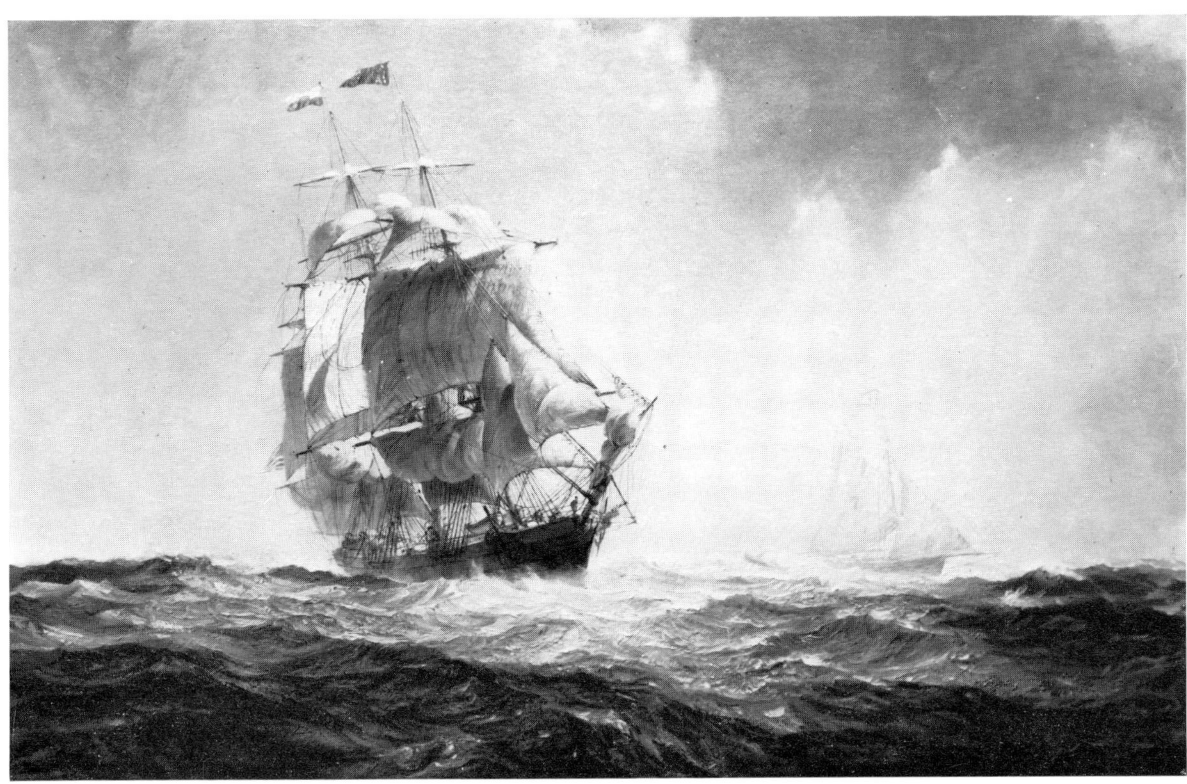

Cat. no. 199 THE CLIPPER 'STAGHOUND' OFF SANDY HOOK Canvas, 40 x 60 ins.

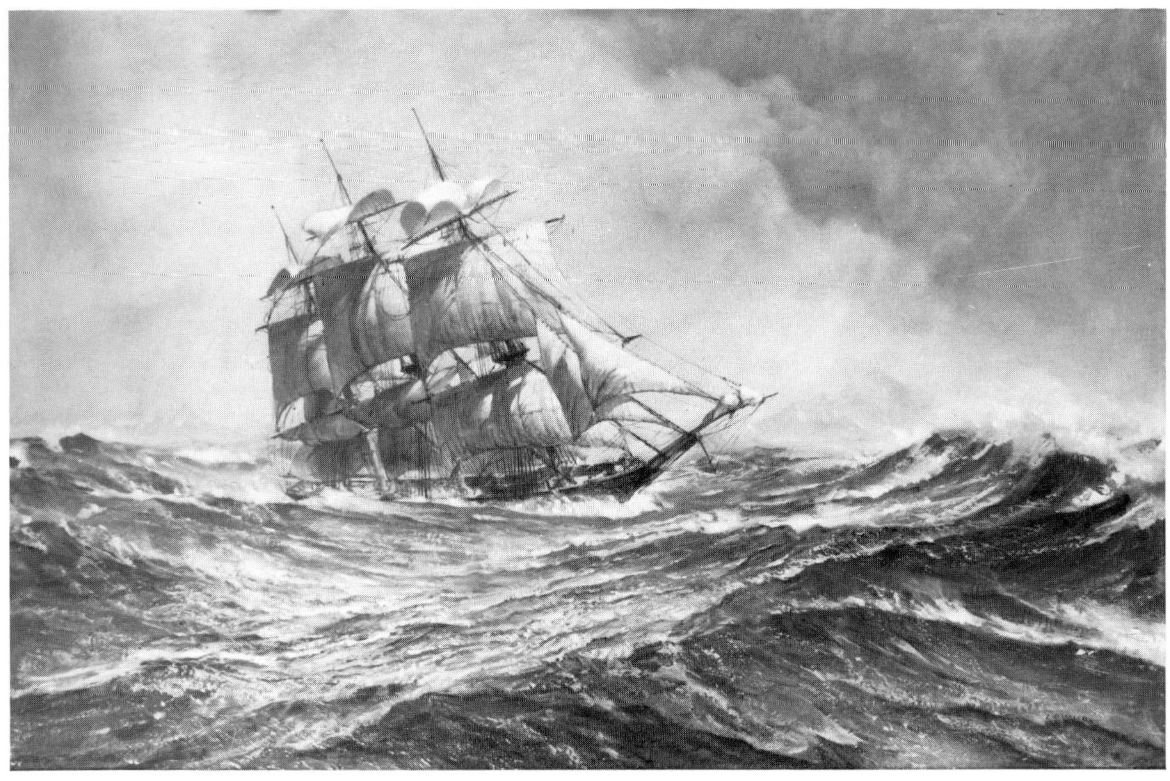

Cat. no. 201 'HERALD OF THE MORNING' ROUNDING CAPE HORN Canvas, 30 x 45 ins.

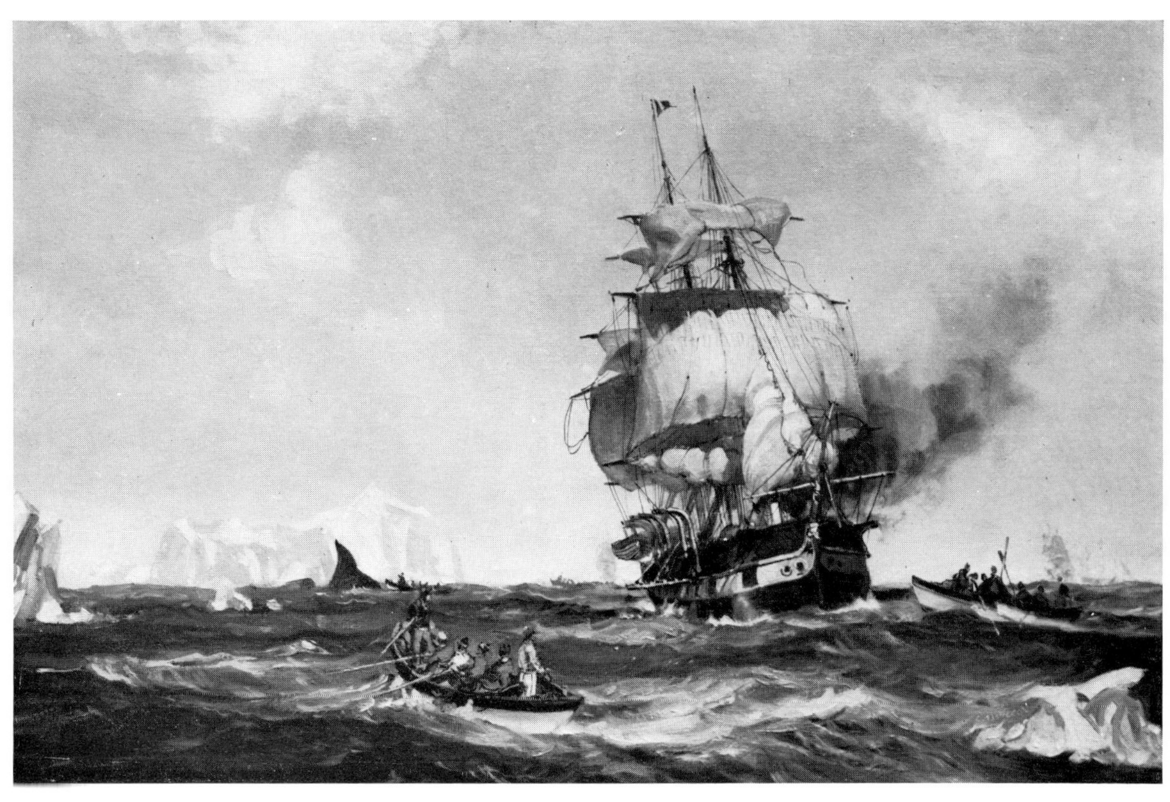

Cat. no. 200 THE WHALER 'JULIAN' OF NEW BEDFORD Canvas, 22 x 30 ins.

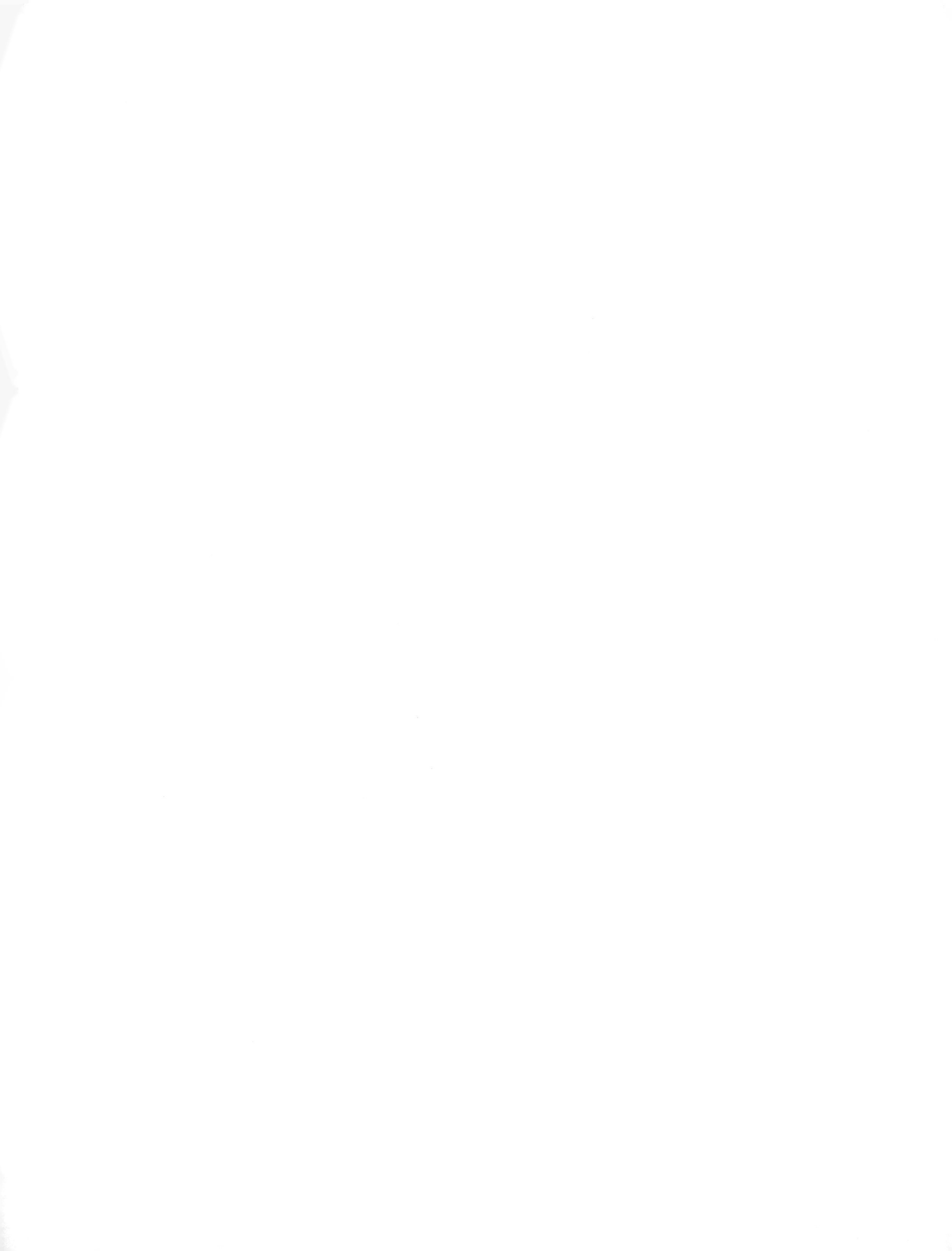

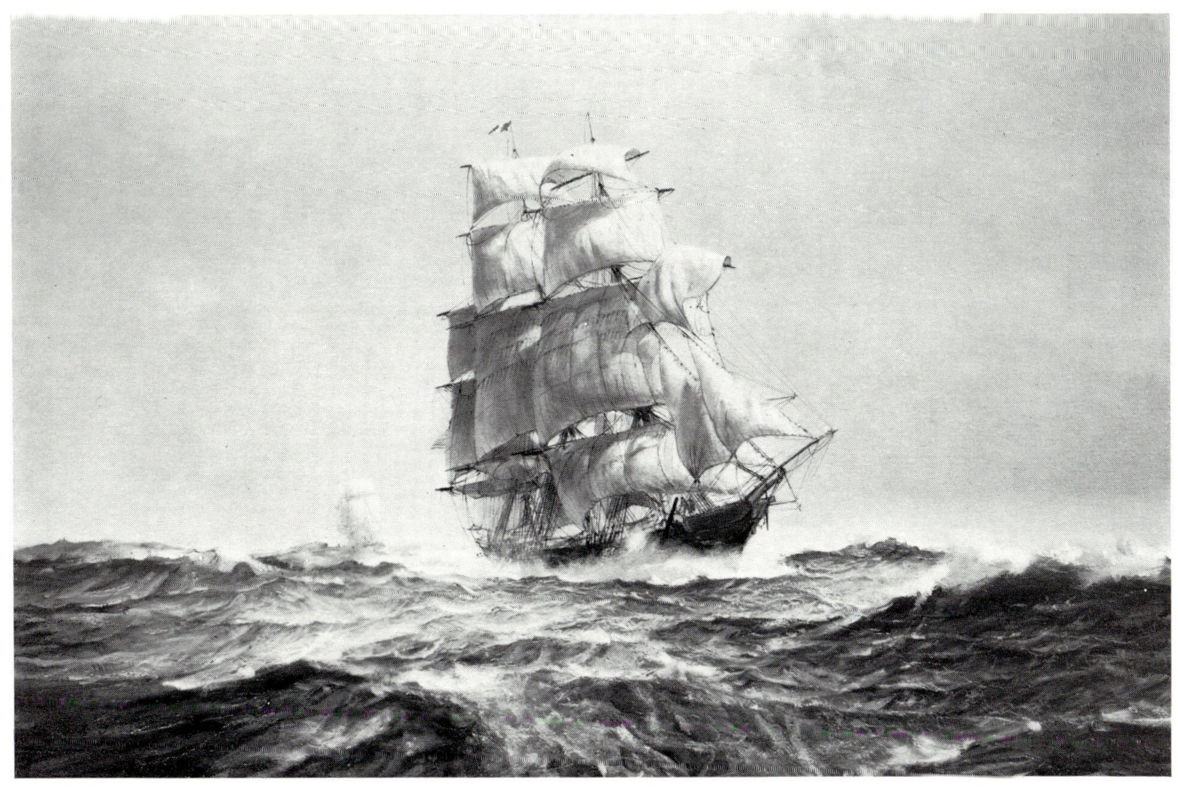

Cat. no. 209 'STARR KING' IN COMPANY WITH 'WITCHCRAFT' Canvas, 30 x 45 ins.

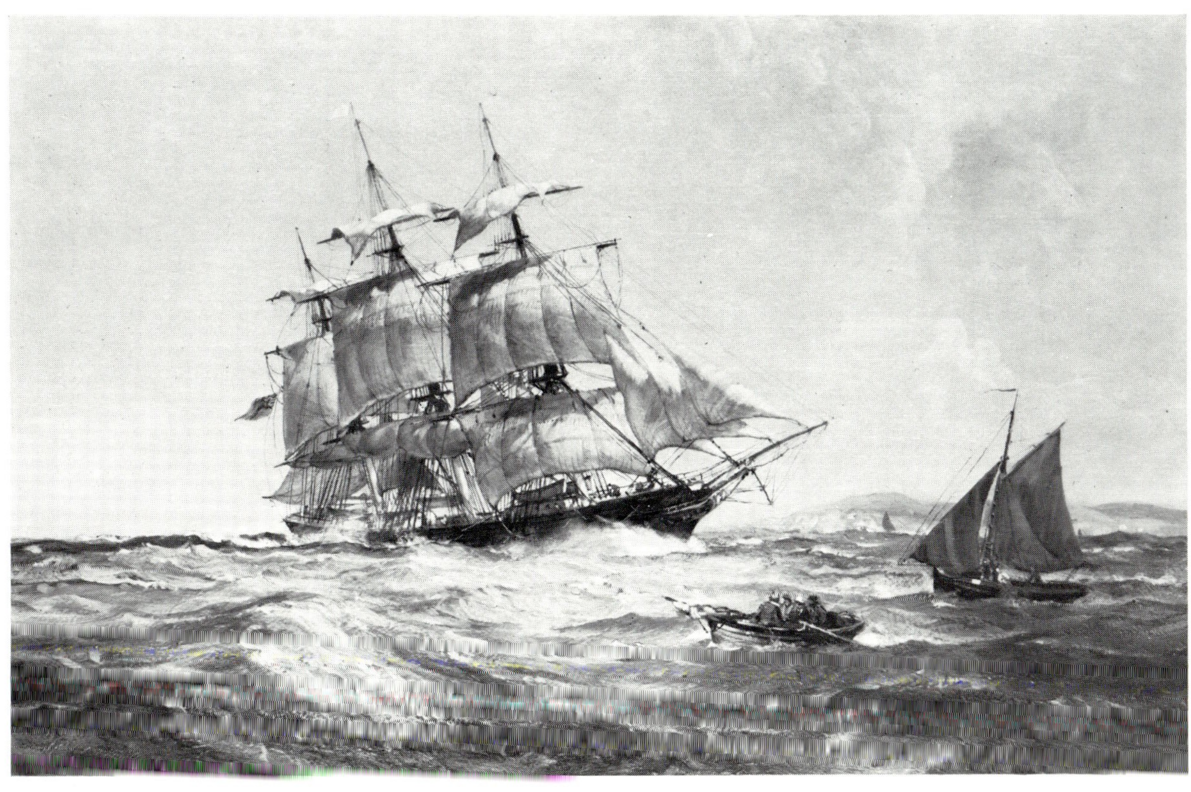

Cat. no. 211 UP CHANNEL – SHORTENING SAIL Canvas, 24 x 36 ins.

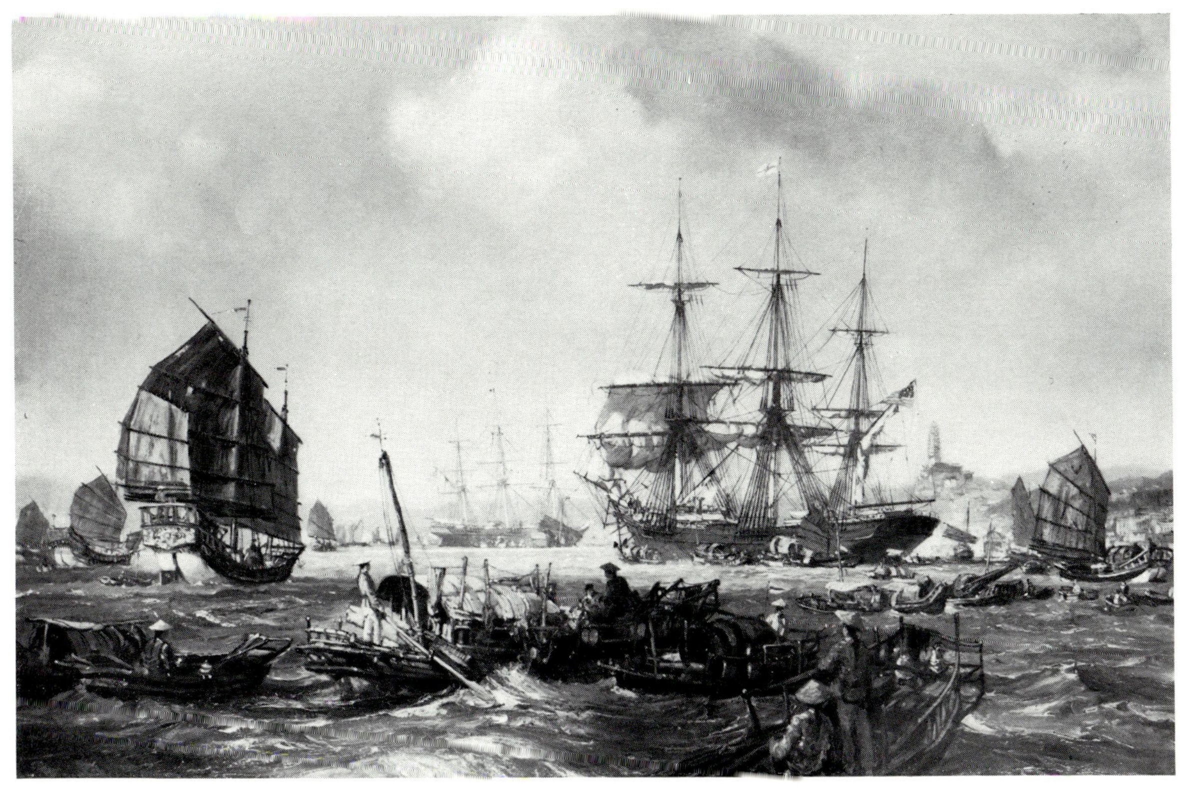

Cat. no. 221 'HIGHFLYER' AT WHAMPOA Canvas, 25 x 40 ins.

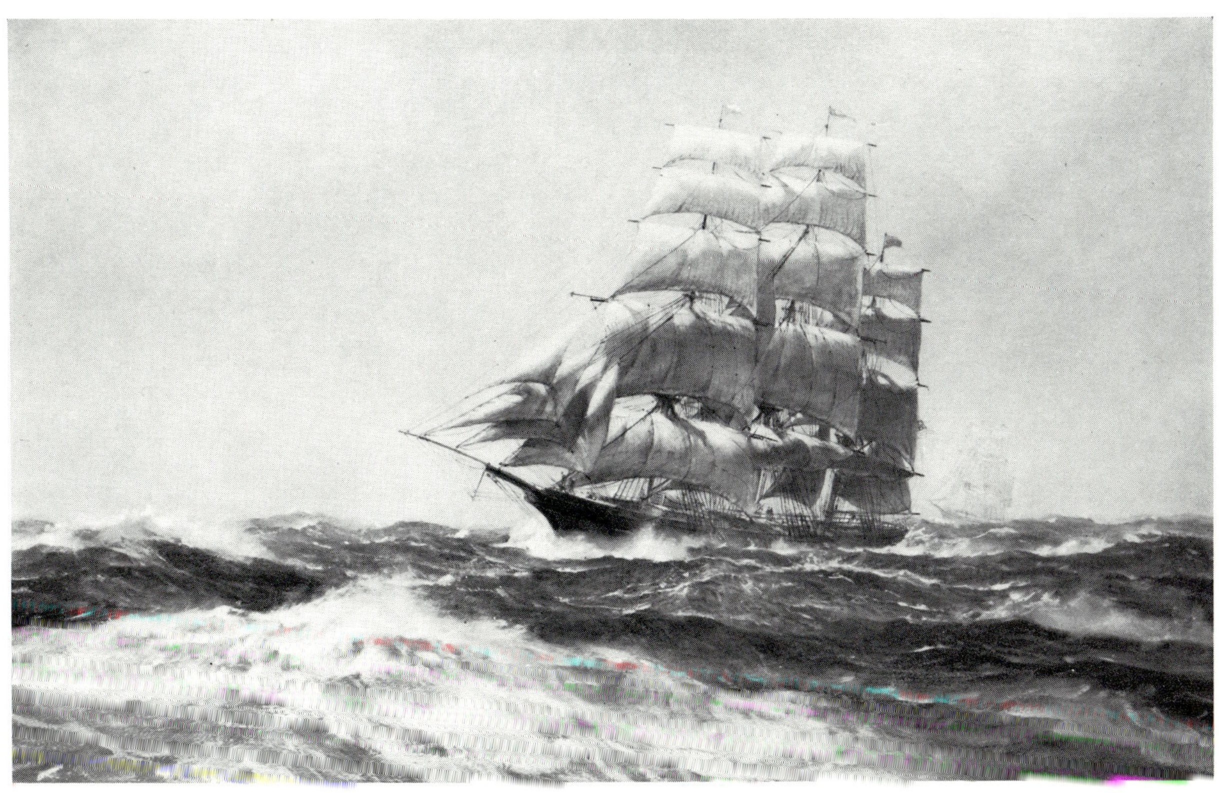

Cat. no. 224 'GAMECOCK' & 'FORMOSA' Canvas, 27 x 40 ins.

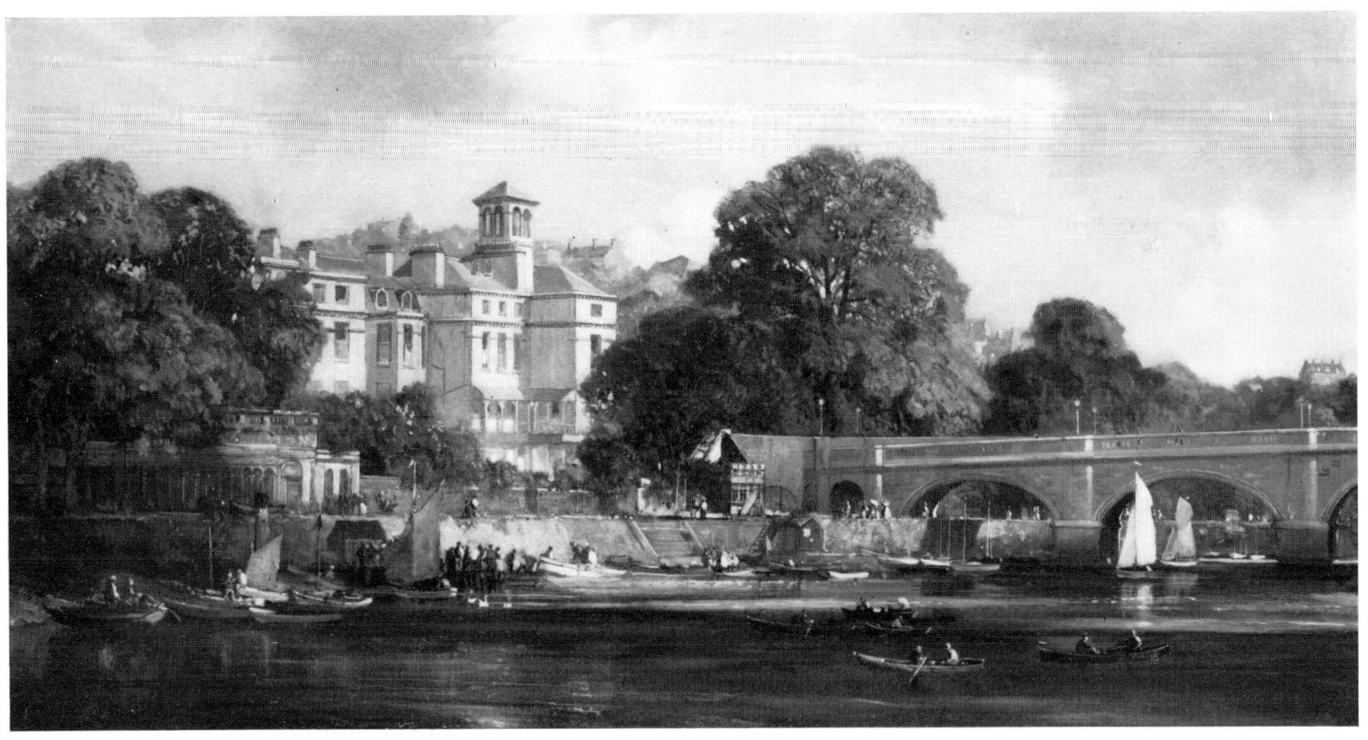

Cat. no. 227 RICHMOND ON THAMES Canvas, 24 x 42 ins.

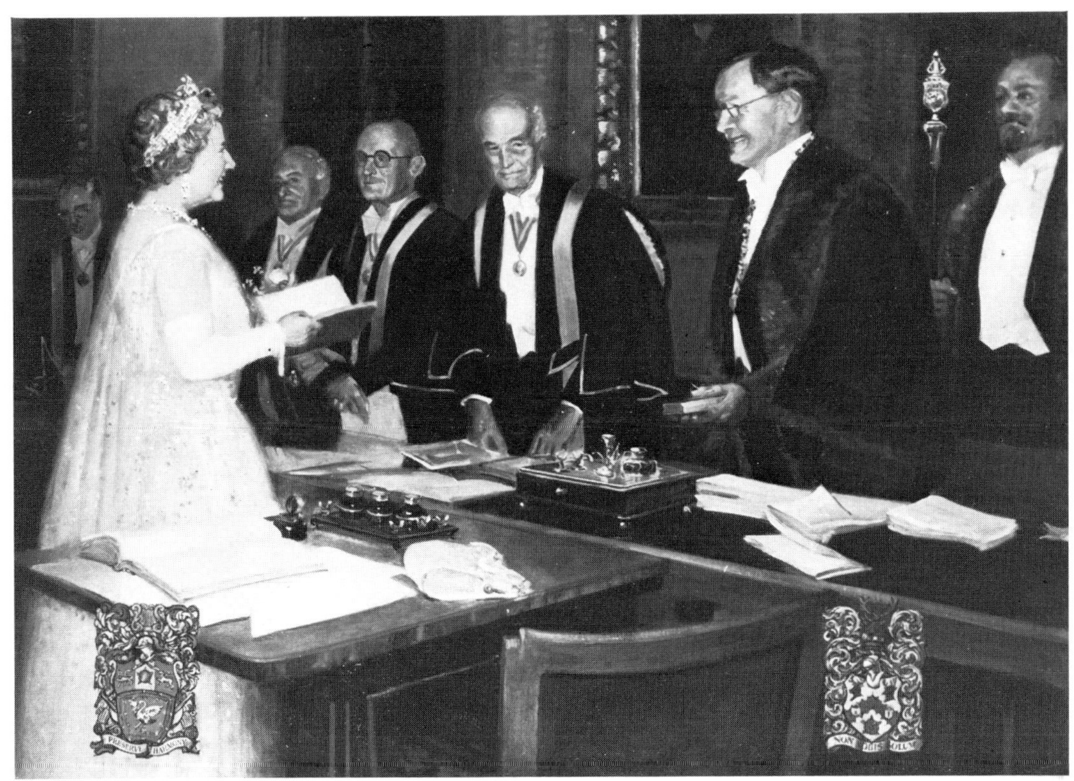

Cat. no. 2[illegible]0 H.M. QUEEN ELIZABETH THE QUEEN MOTHER RECEIVING THE FREEDOM OF MUSICIANS' COMPANY Canvas 30 x 40 ins

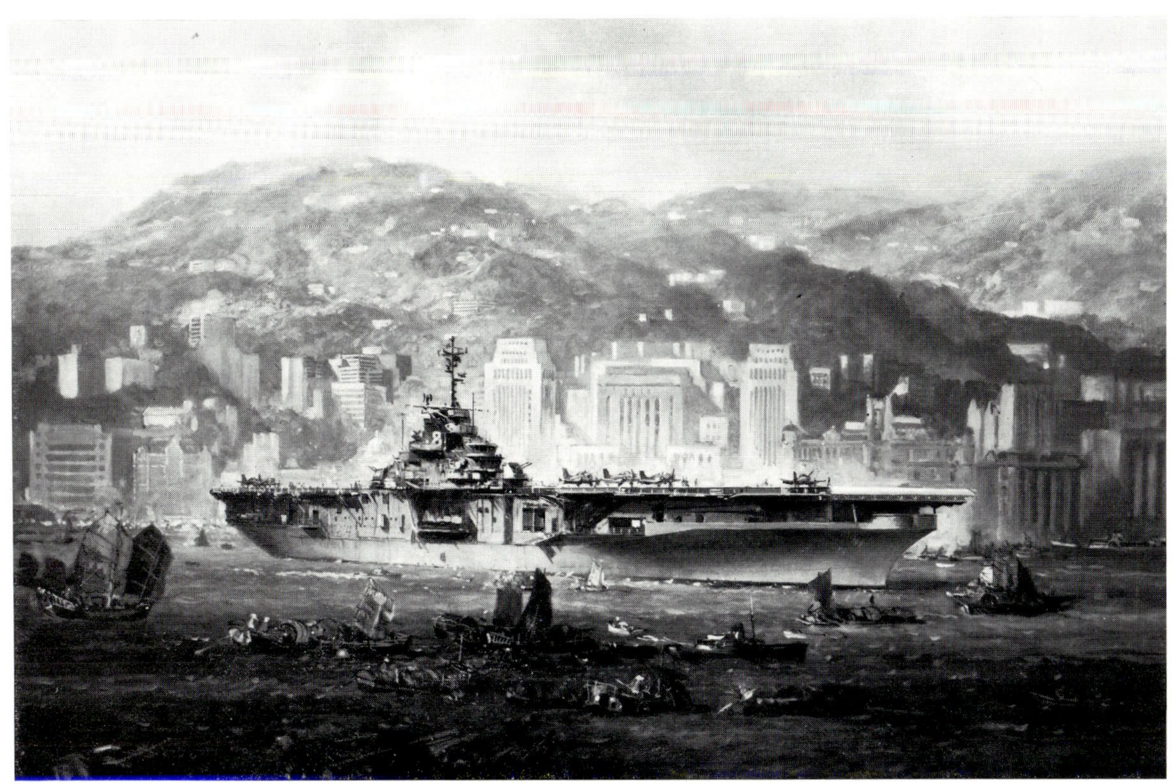

Cat. no. 231 — U.S. NAVAL CARRIER 'VALLEY FORGE' AT HONG KONG — Canvas, 24 x 36 ins.

In the possession of Valley Forge Military Academy

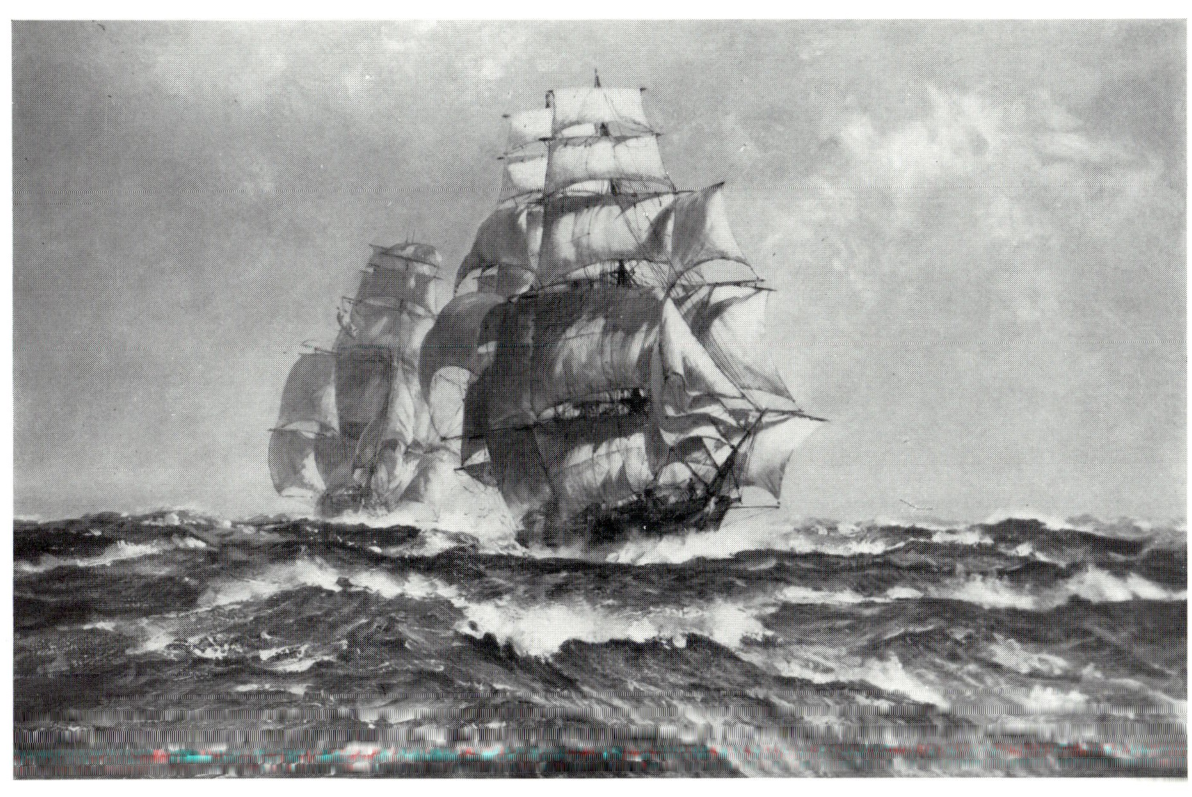

Cat. no. [illegible] — '[illegible]' & 'FORWARD HO' — Canvas, [illegible] ins.

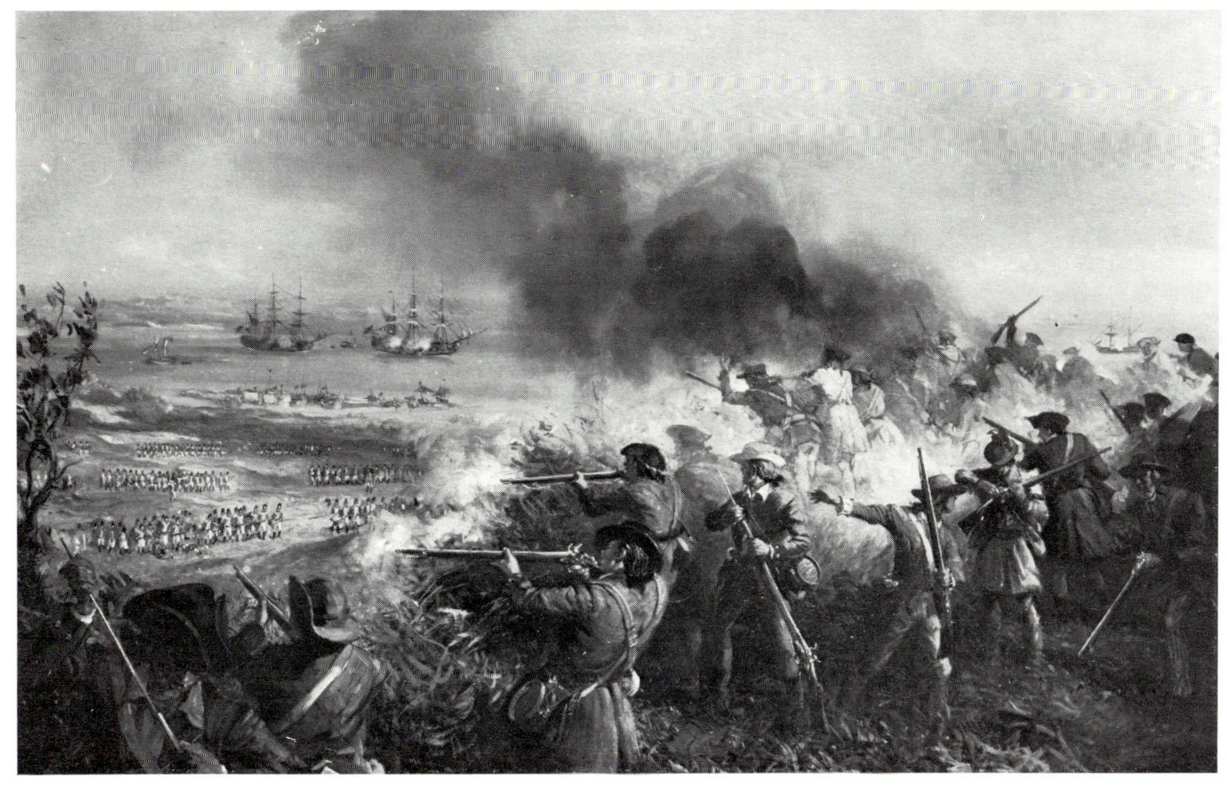

Cat. no. 235 THE BATTLE OF BUNKER'S HILL Canvas, 27 x 40 ins

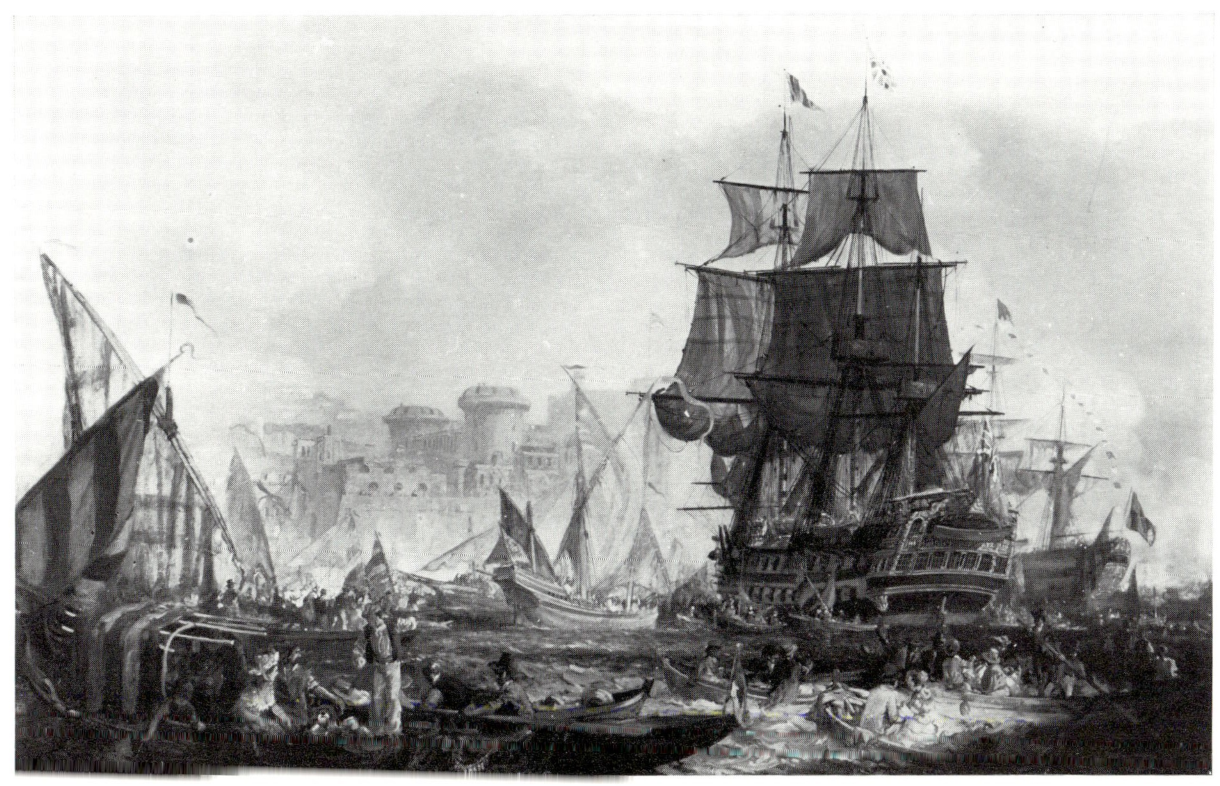

Cat. no. 23[illegible] NELSON IN THE 'VANGUARD' AT NAPLES AFTER THE BATTLE OF THE NILE Canvas, 40 x 60 ins.

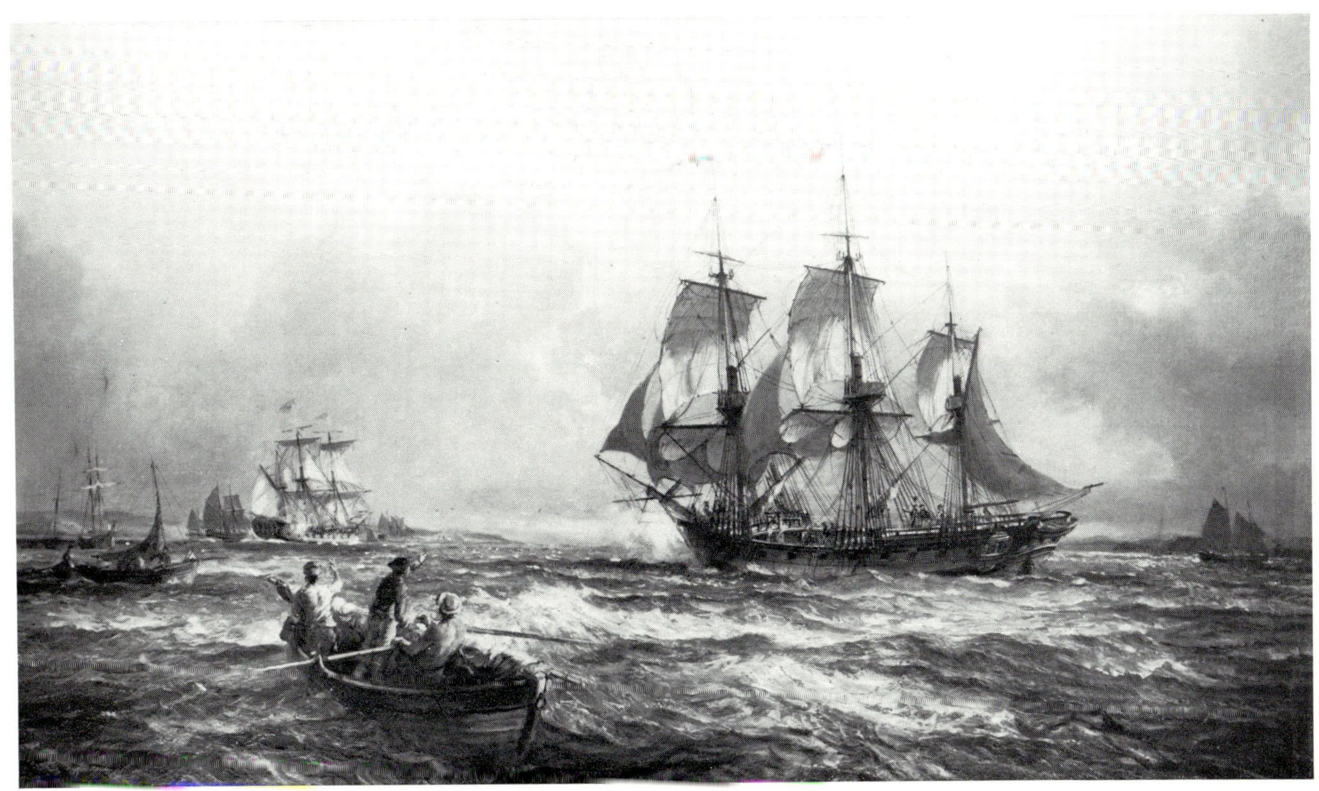

Cat. no. 254 THE 'DEFENCE' IN CHESAPEAKE BAY Canvas, 30 x 50 ins.

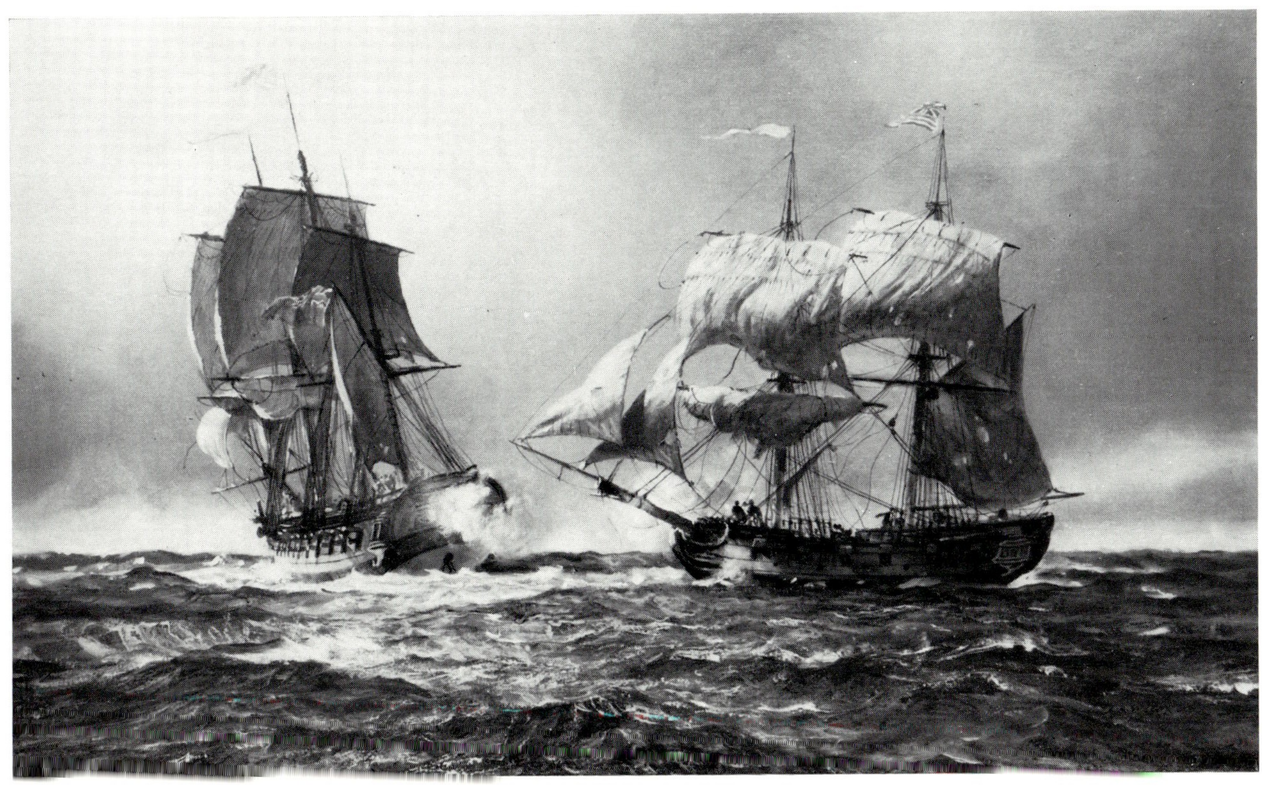

Cat. no. 260 'YANKEE HERO' AND THE FRIGATE 'MILFORD' Canvas, [illegible] x 30 ins.